Praise for *Thank You Power*

"Ever heard the one about being able to catch more flies with honey than vinegar? If you want to eliminate many of the negatives of daily stress and better deal with the realities of your day, then read on. Deborah Norville may have found the real secret to happiness. You'll find the answer inside."

—Dr. Mehmet Oz
Vice Chairman and Professor of Surgery,
Columbia University; and Author, The *You* series

"Deborah Norville has proven that resilience is a big part of success. Success is power—and *Thank You Power* is aptitude and attitude at their most efficient and, therefore, most effective. Deborah has done a wonderful job with a subject that is important for all of us."

—Donald J. Trump

"We should all be grateful that Deborah Norville wrote the inspiring, practical *Thank You Power*. Imagine a self-book that will actually help its readers! She takes academic research on gratitude out of the ivory tower and into the world, doing it justice and adding considerable value to it with compelling stories and realistic advice. Her voice shows through—a smart, sincere, and gracious voice. I recommend this book most highly."

—Christopher Peterson
Professor of Psychology, University of Michigan

"We've all heard it before—count your blessings, concentrate on the positive, say *thank you*—but actually putting it in to practice and becoming a more grateful person can be easily pushed aside in this hurried world. Deborah Norville, in her latest book, *Thank You Power*, clearly lays out easy steps to put you on the path to a more positive lifestyle."

—Anthony Robbins
Best-Selling Author, *Awaken the Giant Within* and *Unlimited Power*

"What a timely message! Deborah Norville has done a masterful job of making a solid case for restoring the character quality of gratitude to American society—and not a moment too soon! I encourage the reading of this book to every man, woman, and young person who desires a richer, more fulfilling life—either personal or professional."

—Zig Ziglar
Author and Motivational Teacher

"People who never complain, groan, or worry don't need this book. (They do need a lesson on honesty.) The other 99 percent of us will benefit from Deborah's practical and hopeful words. We need this message."

—Max Lucado
Pastor, Oak Hills Church; and Best-Selling Author, *3:16*

"Thank you Deborah Norville for offering proof positive of the immense power of gratitude. *Thank You Power* shows each of us that the road to happiness and fulfillment begins with just two simple words and that life is a journey well worth taking."

—Linda Kaplan Thaler
CEO, the kaplan thaler group; and
Coauthor with Robin Koval, *The Power of Nice*

"Your mother was right! You should say *thank you* about almost everything! Why? Because as Deborah Norville's new book proves, being positive and grateful leads to a happier, healthier, more successful life. And by the way, thank you for reading this, and thank you, Deborah, for writing this book."

—Joan Rivers
Entertainer

"This book beautifully illustrates how the depth of our gratitude stems from the depth of our understanding of the people who surround and bless our lives. A remarkable work from a remarkable woman who lives what she teaches."

—Stephen R. Covey
Author, *The 7 Habits of Highly Effective People* and
The 8th Habit: From Effectiveness to Greatness

"Manners aren't ever out of fashion . . . even living on a fast track, we need to take time each day to slow down and be people of grace and gratitude. In *Thank You Power* Deborah Norville explains how taking time to be grateful and acknowledging others with gratitude can be the most important thing you do each day."

—Robert L. Dilenschneider
Chairman and Founder, The Dilenschneider Group, Inc.

"Who wouldn't want to be more optimistic and energetic? Who doesn't want to think more clearly and bounce back from adversity? Who knew feeling grateful could make those things happen? Deborah Norville's new book offers proof of what most of us suspected—our expressions of gratitude are as much a gift to ourselves as they are to those we bestow them upon."

—Nancy G. Brinker
Founder, Susan G. Komen for the Cure

"My mother used to say that the world would be a much better place if people would say *thank you* more often. Drawing on uplifting stories of people from all walks of life, Deborah Norville shows that an attitude of gratitude not only makes for a nicer world but also makes you a happier person."

—Ken Blanchard
Coauthor, *The One Minute Manager* and *Lead Like Jesus*

"What a refreshing, positive read! *Thank You Power* makes me want to do everything I can to be grateful for not only the big things but also the sometimes hard details of my life. This is a formula that can make the whole world a happier place in which to live!"

—Harold G. Koenig, MD
Professor of Psychiatry and Behavioral Sciences and
Associate Professor of Medicine, Duke University Medical Center

"It seems no one wants to say *thank you* these days. Instead, we live with a sense of entitlement—from the child who expects an A on his report card, without the test scores to back it up, to the office worker who wants a promotion despite lackluster performance. In *Thank You Power* Deborah Norville proves that gratitude—plain, simply saying thank you—is at the root of happiness. Following the specific steps she outlines will help you be able to cultivate this power and begin to put it to work in your own life."

—Jake Steinfeld
Chairman and CEO, Body by Jake Global;
Founder, Major League Lacrosse; and Founder, Exercise TV

THANK YOU POWER

OTHER BOOKS BY DEBORAH NORVILLE

Back on Track
I Don't Want to Sleep Tonight
I Can Fly

THANK YOU POWER

Making the Science of Gratitude Work for You

Deborah Norville

THOMAS NELSON
Since 1798

NASHVILLE   DALLAS   MEXICO CITY   RIO DE JANEIRO   BEIJING

Published in Nashville, Tennessee, by Thomas Nelson. Thomas Nelson is a trademark of Thomas Nelson, Inc.

Thomas Nelson, Inc. titles may be purchased in bulk for educational, business, fund-raising, or sales promotional use. For information, please e-mail SpecialMarkets@ThomasNelson.com.

Scripture quotations marked KJV are from the Holy Bible, King James Version.

Scripture quotations marked NKJV are taken from the New King James Version®. © 1982 by Thomas Nelson, Inc. Used by permission. All rights reserved.

Scripture quotations marked NASB are taken from the New American Standard Bible®, © 1960, 1962, 1963, 1968, 1971, 1972, 1973, 1975, 1977, 1995 by The Lockman Foundation. Used by permission.

ISBN: 978-0-7852-8961-6 (trade paper)

Library of Congress Cataloging-in-Publication Data
Norville, Deborah.
  Thank you power : making the science of gratitude work for you / Deborah Norville.
      p. cm.
  Includes bibliographical references.
  ISBN: 978-0-7852-2193-7 (hardcover)
  ISBN: 978-0-7852-8945-6 (IE)
  1. Gratitude. I. Title.
BV4647.G8N67 2007
179'.9—dc22

2007018041

Printed in the United States of America
08 09 10 11 12 RRD 5 4 3 2 1

For Momma and for Daddy,
who taught me thank you first
and
for Niki, Kyle, Mikaela, and Karl,
who give me reason
to say it every day.
Thank you.

If you enjoy feeling frustrated on a
regular basis, if you prefer to look at life
as a series of days simply strung together
and then you die, then please don't waste
your time or money on this book.

But . . . if you are looking to tap into
your personal power to savor life, enjoy
the moment, and effortlessly handle
the challenges that inevitably will
come your way . . . read on.

You'll say, "Thank you,"
and
your life will never be the same.

Contents

Introduction

THIS BOOK WAS BORN OF COMMON SENSE. NOT THAT I claim to have more of it than anyone else. But it just seemed common sense to me—a hunch, really—that if you want to be happy, focus on what you've *got*—not what you've *not*. The benefits of doing just that read like the claims of some too-good-to-be-true infomercial:

- You'll be more optimistic.
- You'll exercise more.
- You'll think more creatively.
- You'll bounce back from adversity faster.
- You'll be less intimidated by challenges.
- You'll have higher immune response.
- You'll be more alert and interested.
- You'll be more adventurous.
- You'll live longer.
- You'll be more likely to help others.
- You'll be more likable.
- You'll be more tolerant.
- You'll be a better boss or team leader.
- You just might do better on a test.

These outcomes, reported in the country's top psychology journals, are the findings of some of the nation's foremost researchers in a newly emerged field called *positive psychology*. For nearly two years, I have been digesting this scientific literature, trying to discover if my hunch had any basis in fact. Did it ever!

Man has been searching for happiness since the beginning. It's one of our *inalienable rights*, isn't it? Right there in the Declaration of Independence, just after *life* and *liberty*. Goodness knows we've been pursuing it long enough: from Eve's first taste of the apple to the conquistadores' quest for golden treasure and the modern-day prowl for a mate, the end game of most of man's endeavors has been fulfillment.

On Wall Street, people in pinstripes rush madly for money and power. Park Avenue plastic surgeons' offices (and plenty of them elsewhere in America) are jammed with ladies, all hoping the latest potion or procedure will make them younger looking and, therefore, happy. A teen races to score the most points and win the MVP trophy. But trophies tarnish; someone else will always have a bigger bank account; and as the poets pointed out long ago, beauty fades. Here we are, two hundred-plus years after beginning the American pursuit of happiness, still chasing it, wondering what the secret is to finding it.

What if—just as in *The Wizard of Oz*, when Dorothy learned that the ability to get home to Kansas had been hers all along—the secret to lasting happiness was within each of us? What if a lasting sense of completion, an enduring feeling of contentment, was possible—simply by changing the lens through which we viewed daily life? Nothing dramatic, nothing painful—no calories expended: just a conscious alteration of the way we look at our own little corner of the world.

Here's the good news: you've got the power right now. Regardless of your age, religion, financial circumstances, or any other classification society might dream up, you have *within you* the tools to allow you to live the life of satisfaction, security, and optimism you long for. That power begins with two words: *thank you.*

When I was a child, my parents were constantly carping at me, "Debbie, say thank you." Yours probably did likewise, and now, as a parent, I do the same—constantly reminding *my* children to be polite. I want them to say, "Thank you," and "Oh no, you first" and to act as well-brought-up, mannerly children. It's what one does in a civilized society.

But society these days seems uncivilized. A sense of entitlement is found everywhere, from the child who expects an A on his report card, without the test scores to back it up, to the office worker who wants a promotion despite lackluster performance. Manners are regarded as a relic of the old days. Who hasn't been annoyed by the loudmouth with the cell phone on the commuter train or shocked when a guest forgets to say thank you?

It's not that we don't have plenty to be thankful for. Americans enjoy an unprecedented standard of living: in the last fifty years, the average family has acquired more and fancier cars, better houses, and more stuff. But more doesn't mean happier. The number of Americans who say they are "very happy" has dropped a bit from 35 to 30 percent,[1] despite all the getting we've been doing.

Americans on average *do* have more money than they did fifty years ago, but after financial stability has been achieved, *more* money doesn't equal greater happiness. According to a report in

Money magazine, if you make $50,000, you're about twice as likely to say you're very happy as someone who makes less than $20,000. But from $50,000 in income to $90,000, there is virtually no increase in happiness level. Forty-two percent of those earning between $50,000 and $89,999 say they are very happy while 43 percent of those earning more than $90,000 also rate themselves as very happy.[2] Divorce, suicide, and depression rates, however, do rise. Is there a connection?

I'm a collector of quotes and often ask people if they have a line or two that has special meaning. Steve Forbes, scion of the *Forbes* magazine family, told me that his favorite quote is the one that appears on his editorial page in his family's business publication:

> *With all thy getting get understanding.*
> —Proverbs 4:7 (kjv)

Get understanding. How interesting that a man behind a magazine focused on wealth accumulation is really just trying to make sense of our world. I think that's probably what pushed me down the career path I chose.

As a television reporter for nearly three decades, I've been sharing the stories of ordinary Americans, trying to make sense of the situations in which my story subjects have found themselves. It's not always easy: The mother of the brain-damaged accident victim. The family of the teen killed by a drunk driver. The woman battling a life-threatening disease. But I have always marveled that certain people, even in the face of heart-stopping obstacles and the most difficult of circumstances, are able to go forward with smiles on their faces and optimism in their outlooks.

As a reporter, you look for the anomaly: the fact that seems a bit off, the story that just doesn't fit. And it didn't make sense to me that, over and over again, people in absolutely the worst imaginable situations seemed relentlessly optimistic. They looked for the better day to come and expected it with certainty.

How was this possible? In each instance, it ultimately came down to the same answer: they were grateful. In each of their sometimes heartbreaking situations, they had found something for which they could be thankful, because being thankful was a long-held habit.

Those "Debbie, say thank you" admonitions from my mom and dad resonated in my memory. Mom was always *awfully* nice to me when I'd hand to her my birthday thank you notes to mail. "Good girl," she'd say as she ruffled my hair. I would bask in the praise, knowing that I was in Mom's good graces for the rest of the day. It was a good place to be. As a child, I spent plenty of time in the doghouse, so I treasured those good days.

Frankly, saying thank you, mentally as well as verbally, was probably a better way to go through life than barreling through the days as a crabby old grouch (though I have plenty of *those* days too!). We all heard it growing up: "You catch more flies with honey than vinegar." But it wasn't just that *other people* appreciated hearing me say thank you. *I* was different. I was better. I just always seemed to *feel happier* on those days when I actually made a point of savoring the aroma of the coffee vendor's cart as I walked past or noticing how beautiful the flowers in the garden were.

Of course, you have to *see* the flowers first.

Most of us blast through each day, virtually unaware of what goes on around us. Think about your daily commute to work. If you are the average American, you spend 24.3 minutes a day getting to your job. Double your trip in and you've spent close to an hour or more each day in transit. I don't know any average Americans, I guess, because everyone *I* know spends much more time than that getting to work. Before I moved, my commute was an hour and a half one way. My sister spends thirty minutes in the car just to get her kids to school, then turns around and goes the *other* way to get to work.

Quick—ten minutes into your daily commute, what do you see outside the window? Come on. You pass by that spot every day! It's not that you aren't aware of the shops and homes along your route. You just don't notice them. Maybe you should.

Common sense was telling me that one aspect to feeling good about life is *noticing* certain things about your life—and acknowledging the good stuff. To the skeptic in me, that *ac-cen-tu-ate the positive* seemed more like a motto for some Dr. Feelgood guy on daytime TV rather than a meaningful standard for a life marked by contentment. Oprah's been talking about her gratitude journal for ages, so it wasn't really anything new. But it did seem like the perfect topic for one of those motivational speakers who have plenty of platitudes about attitudes. Like those late-night infomercial salespeople, they get you all revved up, but in truth, it's just a bunch of hot air. Me, skeptical? *That* was an understatement.

Still, that hunch about injecting conscious appreciation into my daily routine made sense. But journalists don't go on hunches alone. They act on their instincts and follow up on their hunches with investigation to see where their research leads them. I was stunned by what I found when I started snooping. Turns out, I wasn't the only person with this hunch. I discovered a new field of dispassionate, scientific research investigating the impact that mind-set and positive emotions play in our lives. The influence is quantifiable—both physically and emotionally: Practicing gratitude, acknowledging the blessings in your life, and making it a point to recognize those good things, will *positively change your life.* You will be happier, healthier, and better able to handle the stresses of daily life simply by saying thank you.

For years, science has looked at what happens to human beings when things go wrong. We know how bad stress is for us. The negative effects of stress and anger on the cardiovascular system, among other body systems, are well documented. Less is known about what happens when all is right with your world. Turns out the opposite of stress—that is, experiencing *positive* situations and recognizing them as such—can result in a host of encouraging outcomes, from fewer illnesses and higher immune response to more expansive thinking and creative problem solving. That's not a hunch. It's laboratory proven. As I lost myself in my research, I found myself asking, is it possible that the key to real-life happiness can be found in just two words?

Before I took the first step in starting my research, I conducted a little experiment to test-drive my hypothesis. What happened during my experiment knocked me out.

AN EXPERIMENT IN GRATITUDE

Sometimes luck comes when you need it. Every now and then, I mess up on the finances. My mother used to call it having too much *month* at the end of the *money*. It happened in college when I ran out of money and lived on cornflakes through exams. It happened when I got my first apartment and bounced a rent check. More recently, school tuitions were due, but I was still paying off construction bills on our new house. The only reason I hadn't bounced a check was because I was smart enough not to write one.

I had one of those desperate conversations with God about "How will I get out of this financial pickle?" God answered in the form of a last-minute call to give a speech in place of a network news friend who was stuck on assignment. Fortunately, I had the day off and was able (and grateful) to say yes.

The sun was shining, the sky a brilliant blue, and the speech and subsequent question-and-answer session went off without a hitch. I made it to the airport for the trip home with plenty of time to spare.

I was feeling pretty good. *Thank You, Lord!* I silently prayed, grateful that my money worries had been lessened. I looked out the window at the West Virginia mountains. They were the same mountains that had been there when I arrived a few hours earlier, but I hadn't noticed them then. The rounded tops of the Appalachians looked like an undulating green carpet. It reminded me of the mountains where I grew up in north Georgia. I felt an overwhelming, truly physical wave of emotion pass over me. You have no idea how thankful I was for that fill-in work.

Thank You for it all! I silently intoned. In my mind, I heard an old song that we used to sing at camp: *The Lord is good to me, and so I thank the Lord . . . for giving me the things I need, the sun and the rain and the apple trees. The Lord is good to me.*

The Lord has *been good to me*, I thought as I boarded the plane.

I guess I jinxed it.

I don't know about you, but the way it seems to work in my life is, when things are good—something happens. Usually *not* good.

There I was, on the first leg of my flight home; everything was right with my world. Then the storm clouds moved in. Literally. I had just sat down on my connecting flight to New York City when—*BAM!*—roaring thunder and menacing black clouds appeared out of nowhere. The sky grew dark. The winds picked up. The airport shut down. People's *true* nature came out, and it wasn't pretty.

Airport personnel herded us off the plane. Angry mobs surrounded harried gate agents, who simply had no answers to the questions fired their way: "When is the next flight?" "What time will the airport open?" "How will I make my connection in Chicago?"

IN EVERY THING GIVE THANKS

As I stood in line (more of a crush of people than a line, really), trying to retrieve my ticket for the flight that wasn't going anywhere, a verse from the Bible kept echoing in my head. "Say thank you, Deb," it seemed to insist. Creeping forward in line, I was simultaneously trying to book an alternate flight on my cell phone. In front of me was a group of business types who'd been seated near me on the plane. They looked as if they, too, were experienced at dealing with these kinds of frustrations. We smiled at one another and chuckled, saying, "Could be a long day!"

To say that the lined inched forward would be overstating it. The line didn't budge. About the only thing that *was* moving was my blood pressure, which began to rise as I listened to the annoying music the airlines play as you languish on hold. Yet very clearly over that canned music, over the rumble of frustrated travelers, I heard again the words of 1 Thessalonians 5:18: "In every thing give thanks . . ." (KJV).

Man, God is playing mind games with me! I thought.

Not much to be thankful for right about now, but, what the heck? Say thank you, I admonished myself. *Thank you for what?* I pursed my lips and thought. *What on earth can you possibly say thank you for right now? For Pete's sake, you're stuck in Pittsburgh, the airport is shut down, and ain't nobody going anywhere anytime soon!* It took a couple of moments of thinking to come up with something. I'd already said thank you for the financial life preserver, so that didn't count.

OK: Lord, thank You for not letting my flight take off. I could've been killed. I'd covered my share of plane crashes and knew the deadly power of wind shears, so *Thanks, God, for not rushing my obituary* seemed good enough for the moment.

I came to the front of the line. A now-grounded flight attendant was pinch-hitting alongside the gate agents. She looked absolutely wiped out. I felt bad for her and said, "Well, look at it this way: when the plane finally *does* take off, those passengers will be so happy, no one will give you any grief."

She flashed an appreciative smile and said, "That's what I'm hoping," as she handed my ticket back to me. Not that I'd be using it soon. The TV monitor was showing a huge line of thunderstorms that had shut down much of the Northeast. I optimistically booked myself on a later flight.

On my way to the gate (naturally, the farthest possible), I passed the group of advertising people, having a beer and a hamburger. I smiled their way, and they waved me over to join them. "We've just reserved a private jet to get us up to Teterboro" (a private airport outside of New York City), one of them said.

"Want to join us?" offered another.

I was floored. It's not every day you are offered a ride on a private jet.

"Gosh," I stammered. "That's incredibly nice of you, but my company would never authorize that." All right, I wasn't there on TV business, but even if I had been, the studio would never OK travel on a private plane.

"No problem," said the first fellow as he took a sip of beer. "Our clients need us back, and the seat would be empty otherwise. Just come on and join us."

This had never happened to me before. I wondered if this amazing offer had anything to do with my conscious effort to be nice and grateful during the airport chaos.

"You know what? I'd love to!" I accepted. "But there's a rumor there might be a flight down the corridor that's headed to LaGuardia, which is closer to where I need to be. I was just headed down there to check it out." I pulled out my notebook and pen. "Let me get your cell number and let you know if it's for real. If it is, maybe you want to grab seats on that one?"

The one who seemed to be the boss replied, "Naw, we're on the hook for the jet either way. But if it doesn't work out, just let me know, and we'd be happy to have you ride up with us." He handed me his business card before we said good-bye.

I walked—floated, really—down the corridor. How astonishing was this? In the madness, a group of total strangers had offered to help me. For no reason, nothing expected in return. All I'd done was be a bit pleasant. One more thing to be grateful for. One more quick conversation with the man upstairs.

"That was really cool, God. Thanks for the ride." I actually said it out loud. So what if I looked crazy, talking to myself?

By the time I got to the gate, I was exhausted. It was a lot farther than I'd expected, and—surprise!—the flight *didn't* exist after all. But this time, I wasn't grumpy.

Friendly, gratitude-filled Deborah paused a moment. "Figures the flight wouldn't really be leaving," I said as I rubbed my aching feet, "because you are practically the last gate here!" I put my shoe back on and started to leave. "Well, I needed the exercise anyway," I said cheerfully as I turned.

"Hey, wait!" the airline lady called after me. "It's not posted, but there's a flight they've added that's headed up to Westchester Airport. It's not LaGuardia, but it's close."

I have so many frequent-flier miles that the airline sends me mixed nuts at Christmastime. But *this* has never happened to me. A *second time* I'm getting unsolicited help at an airport? I was starting to get a little freaked.

"You are kidding," I said incredulously.

"Nope," she said, "and if you hurry, I think you can make it. I'll call to the gate and let them know you're coming."

She shooed me off in such a hurry that I didn't get her name. Whenever someone goes out of his or her way for me during travels, I try to write a letter to the airline. Someone told me once that the person being complimented gets free tickets or something for his or her family. Anyway, it's a nice thing to do.

I hustled to the gate and, sure enough, the secret flight was about to take off. There was only one seat left—which I got, thanks to the gate person's advance call. I handed my ticket over and received a boarding card for seat 33D. You know the one: last row on the aisle, next to the stinky bathroom! I was thrilled to sit there! At last—I was headed *home*.

The flight attendant at the back commented, as I stowed my stuff in the overhead compartment, "Your travel agent must really hate you. You've got the smelly seat that doesn't recline!" She was smiling as she spoke.

"Are you nuts?" I countered. "I am overjoyed to be sitting here. Heck, I'd sit on the toilet if it had a seat belt. I've run all over this airport to find anything that was headed anywhere close to New York!"

She then went on to assist other passengers, one of whom was a woman who was so rude and dismissive to her that I felt as though *I* should apologize—which I did.

"I am so sorry she acted that way," I said as the angry passenger huffed into her seat. "She must be an amateur. A regular flier would never have been like that." The rude battle-ax seemed to hold the flight crew responsible for the hideous weather. "You don't deserve that," I said to the harried flight attendant. I didn't know what else to say, but it really ticked me off to see the attendant being so verbally abused.

"Thanks." She shrugged it off. "It goes with the territory. We know to expect it on days like this."

I don't think I could do this job, I thought. *I would never be able to deal with people like* that *passenger.*

Then I began to daydream about the good fortune—blessings, really—I'd had that day, both big and small. From the speech that came just when I needed it, to the *nice* people from the ad agency, to the gate agent's inside information, to the pleasant flight attendant who would make sitting in the smelly back row bearable. What could have been an awful day had turned out incredibly well.

The flight attendant interrupted my thoughts. "I'm not asking you; I'm telling you: get your stuff and come with me." She then lowered her voice to a whisper, "There's a free seat up in first class." And she proceeded to take me to it.

She never knew I was holding a first-class ticket the whole time. To think, it all started with "thank you."

In terms of the power of those two words, it was just the tip of the iceberg.

THANK YOU POWER
Make a point to say thank you
to someone today.

one

The Power of
Thank You

Reflect on your present blessings—
of which every man has many—
not on your past misfortunes,
of which all men have some.
—CHARLES DICKENS

SOME DAYS YOU WANT TO JUST STAY IN BED, PULL THE
covers over your head, and hope the world forgets you ever existed.
David Patrick Columbia was having one of those days. New to
New York City, he was completely worn down by the hustle and
bustle of the city that never sleeps. The excitement and pride he'd
felt when he relocated to Manhattan several weeks earlier was
gone. He'd imagined himself the hot young talent about to take
the magazine world by storm. The reality was he was a low-level

assistant, mostly assigned to grunt work on stories about vacuous celebrities with meaningless lives. He couldn't afford a place of his own and knew he was lucky to have a friend on the Upper East Side who didn't seem to mind how long he was a guest in the extra room.

"I was rethinking everything about my move to New York," he recalled. "My ability as a writer, my choice of career—everything." He knew when he relocated to town that it would be a struggle, but he never imagined it would be this hard. That salary that had seemed so attractive when he accepted the job didn't go nearly as far as he'd thought it would. And as nice as his friend was about his extended stay, David couldn't help but feel as if he was sponging off his pal. He felt like Blanche Dubois in Tennessee Williams's *A Streetcar Named Desire*: dependent on the kindness of strangers. The only difference was that he knew the people who were being kind to him.

Against this depressing backdrop, all David wanted to do this Saturday morning was stay in bed and hope it would just get better. But no. *This* Saturday morning, he had to get out of bed and go pick up a photograph that was needed for the next issue. Low man on the roster, it was David's job to hike across town and get it.

It was cold, gray, and damp when David walked out of his friend's apartment building and headed across town. "To this day, I don't know what possessed me to do this, but I decided to start counting things I passed along the way that made me smile," he says. "Maybe it was something someone had told me from an Al-Anon session or something, but for whatever reason, I just told myself I was going to see how many pleasing things I came across as I walked over to Fifth Avenue."

The first thing on David's list: a mother walking her baby, all bundled up in a stroller. "I have always had a soft spot for babies, and that little face just made me smile." Then after that, a movement in the sky caught his eye. It was a jet passing over Manhattan. "Something about flying has always captivated my imagination, and to this day, every time I see a plane in the sky, I just get excited."

And so it went. From the smells of the bistros to the displays in the store windows, each block of David's compulsory crosstown trip found him acknowledging something that brightened his mood. By the time he'd delivered the photo as required, he says he was feeling pretty good—*and* thankful that he'd made the intimidating move to the Big Apple.

"That walk reminded me that I lived in a place that was exciting and interesting and invigorating," he told me. "I often do this whenever I'm feeling down—for some reason, it just makes me feel better." It's been more than twenty years since David took that walk of thanks across Manhattan. Today he's a successful entrepreneur in the media business. His gratitude stroll continues to help him stay focused.[1]

It's easy to say thank you when you've just won the lottery. The words just roll off your tongue when you've been given a big raise or a promotion. Get an incredible piece of jewelry or a new golf club? Thank you. And that second helping of a sinfully delicious, totally calorie-free dessert? Thank you. We live in a society in which the spectacle of saying thank you attracts more than a billion television viewers. That's really what the Academy Awards, the Emmys, and all those other awards shows are, aren't they? Just one big, teary thank you after another, intertwined with an occasional memorable speech or gaffe.

Saying thank you is one of the first things a cooing mother teaches a baby. When times are good, we're good at saying it. We *know* we are supposed to acknowledge what we're given. When a person knows that thank you is going to seen by others, he makes an *extra* effort to say it.[2]

The other day, my son was buried in the sports section at breakfast as I poured the milk on his cereal. He mumbled, "Thanks," and I am quite sure he had no idea he was saying it. *Gracias, merci, tack, obrigado, danke, asante*—you probably can *say* thank you in a zillion languages that you don't speak.

But have you tried *feeling* it, embracing it? You know you embrace all the stuff for which you aren't thankful. If you're like most people, you probably grab hold of life's negatives like a pit bull, and won't let go. "Oh, not *me*," you say. Really? Keep reading.

Chances are something didn't go the way you planned it today. Perhaps something even went hideously wrong. A cross word over breakfast stays with you all day. Your morning starts off on the wrong foot, and the bad feelings just won't leave. Like a bad penny, that unpleasant exchange at breakfast keeps popping up in your mind. Your stomach tightens at the thought; your lips purse. You think of all those things you were too angry or not smart enough to say over the breakfast table. You're much more assertive in those fantasy conversations, and—man!—you're letting him have it, saying all the things you *wished* you'd said.

Aside from breakfast—how was the rest of your day? Not the best, huh? Actually pretty awful? Do you think, just *maybe*, that your no-good, very bad, terrible, *awful* day might have had something to do with your holding on to that morning mix-up like a dog to a piece of meat? The crashing dominoes of things that went wrong all began with that spat over the Cheerios, a spat on which you fixated *all day*.

What if you'd focused on something else? Instead of letting the argument at breakfast dominate your thoughts, what if you'd reminded yourself instead of that automotive magic that got you smoothly to work this morning? Every single light on that usually backed-up four-lane you take daily was green. You sailed through traffic—the most stress-free drive you've had in ages.

How would you have felt at the end of the day if you had let your thoughts be dominated by the memory of the office assistant's face when she received her surprise birthday cake? She was so pleased. It was nice that the lady who does so much for everyone else at work was on the receiving end of something sweet herself.

Did you notice that letter you got from a long-lost friend? Filled with news, tidbits about her life, genuine interest in what you've been doing—reading that letter was like having your friend right there in the same room with you. Reflecting on it, you can't help but feel a smile growing at the corners of your mouth.

Yet you've let yourself plod through the day, ticked off, mad at the world, and probably short-tempered with people who didn't deserve it. All because you just won't stop thinking about that silly dispute at breakfast. Snap out of it!

If you'd spent the day relishing the magic of the easy ride, acknowledging your good fortune to work with such kind and caring people, and being valued by a dear friend, you'd feel pretty good right now. Literally. You'd feel good. There they are: three things today that were positives in life's ledger book. Had you focused on them, you would be happier.

But, nah, you opted to let a squabble over . . . what *was* that argument about, anyway?—wreck your day. You've come home in as foul a mood as you left it.

Fifty years ago, scientists discovered that female silkworm moths put out a powerful sex attractant. "The minutest amount of it [makes] male moths beat their wings madly in a 'flutter dance'" that proves their attraction.[3] Humans may not work the same way, but a few studies seem to indicate that there's a similar chemical-attractant effect in people. What *is* quite clear is that certain human *behaviors* can cause predictable outcomes. Science has proven it.

Spend just a few minutes each day focusing on the good things that happened, the incidents and situations that you'd put in the plus column if you were noting plusses and minuses. You'll be healthier. You'll sleep better and exercise more. You'll feel more optimistic. Take just a moment to note the day's blessings and you'll sense that you have more energy. You will feel more alert and active. Do this for a period of time, and you'll realize you are making progress toward your goals in life. You may even discover you're less of a mess, more organized, less possessive—the clutter that used to collect around you seems to disappear.

BLESSINGS COUNT

The hardest arithmetic to master is
that which enables us to count our blessings.
—ERIC HOFFER

Remember David Patrick Columbia from earlier in the chapter? What he discovered in his own life, Robert Emmons proved in his laboratory. A professor of psychology at the University of

California–Davis, Emmons has long been interested in the role gratitude might play in one's physical and emotional well-being. As a scientist, his world revolves around *proving* what others accept on faith. Gratitude proponents, like Oprah Winfrey, preach that it's a good thing to keep a journal, to take note of your blessings. With a fortune estimated by *Forbes* magazine at $1.4 billion, certainly Oprah's got plenty to be grateful for. But if noting your blessings *is* a good thing, *how much* of a good thing is it?

The short answer? More than you'd ever believe.

"There was a whole lot of better stuff going on!" Speaking from his office at the University of California–Davis's psychology department, Robert Emmons's enthusiasm has an almost hurricanelike force. His career has been devoted to trying to understand what it is that makes people happy.

"I wanted to see if we could actually make people more grateful," Emmons recalled during our interview. He said, "There are a lot of ideas floating around in the self-help literature about how to be happier and how to live an optimal life, but until it's been established scientifically, it means nothing."[4]

The experiment I did during my storm-induced layover at the Pittsburgh airport, Professor Emmons, along with psychology professor Michael McCullough of the University of Miami, conducted in an organized fashion, putting into place the controls and variables that make a study trustworthy. It was brilliant in its simplicity.

The professors took three groups of volunteers and randomly assigned them to focus on one of three things for a week: hassles, things for which they were grateful, or ordinary life events. Group A focused on everything that went wrong or was irritating, such as

"The battery was dead on my car" or "That jerk cut me off on the highway." Group B volunteers honed in on situations that they felt enhanced their lives, e.g., "My boyfriend is so kind and caring; I am lucky to have him" or "That was the most spectacular sunrise; I'm glad I got up early." Group C just remembered events: "I cleaned my closet," or "I went shoe shopping."

Participants were asked to list five examples in their respective categories and then quantify how they felt about what they'd listed: irritated, ashamed, stressed, joyful, grateful, forgiving, calm, proud, etc. They were also asked specific lifestyle questions: How much time do you spend exercising? What physical symptoms do you experience—are you sick, suffering from allergies? Do you feel particularly energetic? If they had received assistance from someone, participants were asked how they felt about it: grateful? annoyed? embarrassed? appreciated? Finally, they were asked how they felt overall, both as they looked back at the past week and as they looked forward to the week ahead.

The people who focused on gratitude were just flat-out happier. They saw their lives in favorable terms. They reported fewer negative physical symptoms, such as headaches or colds, and they were active in ways that were good for them: they spent almost an hour and a half *more* per week exercising than the people who focused on their hassles. In addition, those who'd been on the receiving end of someone else's kindness rated higher in joy and happiness than the others. In short, those who focused on what they were grateful for felt a higher level of gratitude. Life just seemed better for them.[5]

People around them recognized that. Professor Emmons says, "They noticed that the people had more joy, more energy. They could see that they were becoming more optimistic. They even seemed to be perceived as more helpful, you know, going out on a limb to help people." Emmons was surprised by this result. "This is not just something that makes people happy like a positive thinking/optimism kind of thing, but really gets people to *do* something, that is, to become more prosocial or more compassionate or more optimistic."[6] This didn't happen in the other two groups.

Emmons and McCullough took their study further. Rather than focus on hassles, blessings, or events on a weekly basis, they rounded up some volunteers—college students, who received course credit for their participation in the experiment—to do it *every day*. Along with the focus on life events, the researchers asked for specifics: how many alcoholic drinks volunteers had, how many aspirin or other pain relievers they took, the quantity and quality of their sleep—and they wanted folks to compare themselves to others: Are you better or worse off?

If you were going to have dinner with anyone from the study, you'd want someone from the gratitude group at your table. Right off the bat, Emmons and his team recognized that there was something especially impactful about a regular gratitude check. A follow-up study found the effect even more powerful when the gratitude exercises were done on a daily basis. Those who found something to appreciate every day were less materialistic, that is, they were less apt to see a connection between life satisfaction and material things. They were *more* willing to part with their possessions. The bumper sticker that reads "The one with the most toys, wins" was unlikely to be found on any of their cars.

The grateful people were less depressive, envious, and anxious, and much more likely to help others, a fact not lost on those around them. When other people were asked their impressions of the daily-gratitude students, they generally judged them as empathetic, helpful, and prosocial. That is, they felt the members of the gratitude group were more likely to put themselves out for others.

Here's a laundry list of the study's conclusions about test subjects who were consciously grateful:

♦ They felt better about their lives as a whole.
♦ They were more optimistic.
♦ They were more energetic.
♦ They were more enthusiastic.
♦ They were more determined.
♦ They were more interested.
♦ They were more joyful.
♦ They felt stronger about handling challenges.
♦ They exercised more (nearly an hour and a half more per week!).
♦ They had fewer illnesses.
♦ They got more sleep.
♦ They made progress toward important personal goals.
♦ They were more likely to have helped someone else.
♦ They were perceived by others as more generous and helpful.
♦ They were less envious of those with more possessions.
♦ They were less cluttered.[7]

Related studies have found additional benefits, all of which could arguably be linked to a grateful mind-set:

- Clearer thinking—more creativity and openness to ideas[8]
- Better resilience during tough times[9]
- Higher immune response[10]
- Less likelihood of being plagued by stress
- Longer lives[11]
- Closer family ties
- Greater religiousness[12]

Along with thinner thighs and six-pack abs, this is a fairly comprehensive list of what most of us would wish for in life.

"I have studied a lot of topics in the nearly twenty-five years since I've been in graduate school, but there is no topic that has gotten more interest from people than this—and it's exciting," study coauthor Robert Emmons told me. In fact, Emmons says he was pretty jazzed about the research results himself. "From the very beginning, when I first started this research, I was so excited that I couldn't sleep." Emmons is eager to see others begin the practice he studied in the lab. "The challenge," he warns, "is not to make it sound too corny or simplistic or superficial."[13]

Study participants did not know *why* they were doing these exercises. Any changes that were observed were simply conditions the participants noticed as different. I'll explain why that is noteworthy in a moment.

So how does one begin? It is surprisingly and deceptively simple. In fact, if you are over the age of six, you can do it. (Researchers say anyone younger than that is simply incapable of experiencing gratitude.[14]) Thank You Power costs you nothing but a few minutes of your time. But it requires two things of you: consistency and an open mind. (It's OK if you are skeptical about this.)

Professor Emmons also advises dedication. He says, "I think gratitude is a very demanding quality, a rigorous quality we need to work on. It is a discipline, an exercise, and it doesn't come easily to most people." He speaks from experience: "It never came easily to me, either."[15]

THE 3 Rs: REST, REFLECT, WRITE

Take a moment during the day—most people find those last minutes just before retiring to be best—to jot down three things that happened today for which you are grateful. Buy yourself a simple spiral-bound notebook or a fancy journal—what you write *on* doesn't matter. What matters is *what* you write. Use the *Thank You Power Checklist* on the next page to help you get started. What merits inclusion in your notebook? Anything that uplifted you at the time it happened, that brought a smile to your face or your heart. Put another way—something you're glad about, that made you happy today or will contribute toward your future happiness.

After each situation or event for which you feel thankful, write *why* this was good for your life. Perhaps today you received a letter or e-mail from an old school friend who hadn't been in touch for years. Why was this a good thing? Well, it reminded you of the good times you had together way back when. It forced you to realize that people think of *you* even though you've had no contact with them—which must mean you are a pretty special person. It prompted you to think of other long-lost chums and planted the seed that a reunion with the old gang would be really fun to organize. That message from your friend reminded you that it is the people in your life that really give it meaning.

Thank You Power Checklist

1. Thank you for _____

_____

because _____

_____

and (name here) _____ is important
because_____

_____

2. Thank you for _____

_____

because _____

_____

and (name here) _____ is important
because_____

_____

3. Thank you for _____

_____

because _____

_____

and (name here) _____ is important
because_____

_____

Finally, make a note of *who*, if anyone, played a role in what you've recalled for the day and how that person impacted your life. In the case of the letter from the old friend, the who is easy. Maybe you got pulled over by a police officer on the way home from work, but instead of giving you a ticket, he just gave you a warning. Perhaps this evening you are grateful you got off with a warning and that your insurance rates won't be going up. And it's all due to that officer who decided to give you a break.

None of this sounds hard, does it? Given the choice between this exercise and fifty sit-ups plus twenty-five push-ups, you're much more inclined to pick up a pen, aren't you? The reason this works is multifold:

- ◆ It forces your focus onto what went right today, versus the inevitable things that went wrong.
- ◆ It brings you into the present—no more of the *woulda-coulda-shoulda* looking at life but rather a positive, concrete look at your life as it is.
- ◆ It reminds you of the interconnectedness of life. In today's fast-paced world, one can literally go for days without human contact, thanks to ATM machines, which allow us to avoid the bank teller; Internet grocery shopping, which keeps us from standing in line; Web-based bill paying, which helps us avoid the post office; and e-mail, which allows us to connect with people without actually having to talk to them. But though eliminating the human element may make transactions go more smoothly, it also eliminates the rich, emotional aspect of living. This exercise reminds you how much others add to the quality of your life.

♦ It enhances self-esteem. Human nature tells us that good
things should happen to good people. If the good things
on your daily list happened to you, it goes without saying
that you deserved them. The old L'Oreal hair color com-
mercial always ended with ". . . and I'm worth it." Indeed,
you are!

Studies done after Emmons and McCullough's initial experiment have replicated the positive results that come from counting
one's blessings. Some suggest, though, that less may not only be
more, but it may also be better. A study conducted at the University
of California–Riverside found that people who counted their blessings just once a week showed more improvement in well-being
than those who did it three times a week.[16] It could be that participants counting more frequently just got tired of it, making the
practice less meaningful.

SHORT-CIRCUITING THE POWER

Experts also say that your frame of mind when engaging in the
practice is also important. The power of thank you is mitigated if
you use it simply to achieve the benefits I've just detailed. Real
gratitude is an others-focused emotion in which the emphasis is
on the *giver*, not one's own betterment or psychic improvement.
A what's-in-it-for-me attitude will probably leave you disappointed
with what one could call a *Thank You Power outage*. Evidence for
that comes from one study in which participants were asked to listen to Igor Stravinsky's "Rite of Spring." One group was ordered to
cheer themselves up by listening to it. Others were asked to take

note of how happy they felt listening to the music. The third group was told just to listen. The only people who felt happier listening to the song were the people who simply listened. The suggestion that the song might alter one's mood evidently eliminated any possibility that it could.[17]

There are other limits to Thank You Power. It does not make you immune to the cares and perplexities of daily life. Emmons and McCullough found that the people in the gratitude group did not have less pain or experience fewer hassles of daily living. Nor were they less angry, depressed, sad, or otherwise negative. It's just that those things didn't bother them as much.

In other words, they got over their hassles faster, thanks to the strengths they'd developed through Thank You Power. The psychologists suggest that simply focusing on those things for which they were grateful broadened their mind-sets and allowed them to draw on the positives they'd singled out as a source of support while distressed. You'll learn more about how that works in chapter 4.

Niagara Falls has enough waterpower to generate 4.4 million kilowatts of electricity. Left alone, the Niagara is just a spectacular natural wonder. But collected and channeled, the waters of the Niagara River are enough to light 1.7 billion homes. Your daily routine of acknowledging what's good in your life is the beginning of gathering the power you possess but aren't using. As you read on, you'll discover the ways other people have taken Thank You Power and made it an incredible force in their own lives.

> *Men are disturbed not by things, but by the view which they take of them.*
> —EPICTETUS

POWER TEST

Jim Boyles, a financial consultant in Georgia, agreed to give Thank You Power a try. From this exercise, it wasn't unprecedented strength that he first noticed but an unexpected patience with his employees. "I'm not an ogre or anything, but in my business any mistake can cost my clients money. The people who work with me have got to get it right. What I discovered while doing this was that I was a lot less quick to blow up when something went wrong or something wasn't done as quickly as I wanted it done."

Married to his college sweetheart, Jim has one son in college, while the other has recently joined his firm. Jim enjoys showing his son the ropes of the finance business and proudly tells friends how quickly his son passed the required SEC and other necessary exams. Jim's gratitude sheets predictably refer to his appreciation for his wife, his pleasure at having his eldest follow in his footsteps, and his delight in his younger son's academic progress. To his surprise, focusing on his immediate family also gave him a greater appreciation for the people at his office—his work family if you will.

"I realized that I was probably more impatient with them than I needed to be," Jim mused. "Truth be told, it really didn't matter with every single task that every single thing be done that day. I've noticed that I myself have become a lot more easygoing about the less important stuff." Then, as if to point out that he can still be a drill sergeant when it counts, he hastened to add, "But we'll all stay till midnight if we have to to make sure we've got things right for our clients."[18]

Consider how Jim's observations might have positive and lasting consequences in his life. Being less quick on the trigger with his employees can reasonably be expected to result in happier workers. Happier employees are more likely to stay on the job and, as you'll see elsewhere in this book, are apt to be better employees because their work environment is pleasing to them. They are also *prone* to perform better because they know they are valued within the organization.

With Jim always cognizant of his life's blessings, his wife has noticed his increased appreciation of his family. She liked the old Jim just fine, she says, but the new, grateful Jim is a jewel.[19]

After just a few days of keeping a gratitude list, Jim thinks he just might make it a habit.

THANK YOU POWER
List three things for which you are thankful.

two

Hello, *Thank You,* My Old Friend

Gratitude is not only the greatest of virtues,
but the parent of all others.
—CICERO

IT'S NO FUN BEING SICK. IT'S NOT MUCH BETTER BEING a family member of someone struggling with health problems. When I was a child, my mother was in and out of hospitals, first with a spinal problem and later to deal with the ravages of rheumatoid arthritis. It's a helpless feeling for a little kid: watching my mom relearn to walk when I was only eight, hearing her annual Christmas wish for "new arms and legs" when I was a teen. She died when I was twenty.

I have long regretted never getting all those mom-daughter

conversations that other women have had. I have regretted more that I didn't have certain conversations with her doctors. As it turned out, my mother needed a hip replacement. But the X-ray indicating that as the source of her problems wasn't taken until her physical condition was so poor that she was no longer a candidate for surgery. I wish I had badgered the doctors to keep looking for a reason why my mother couldn't walk. But then, what fifteen-year-old knows that you sometimes have to nudge to get results?

Maybe we should have just given Mom's doctors a bag of candy. That's all it took to spur on doctors in one experiment.

After being given just a little bag of candies, the doctors in a study conducted by Dr. Alice Isen were better able to process the facts of some difficult medical cases and come to a correct conclusion while still remaining open to new information that might change their diagnoses. They were also more willing than physicians who didn't get candy to spend time evaluating the patients' charts and to think outside the box about what might be causing their ailments.

Isen is the nation's leading researcher on *positive affect*. For more than thirty years, this Cornell University professor has been looking at the side effects when people feel good. What actually happens? Does a positive, upbeat frame of mind change their abilities in any way? In between her teaching, travel schedule, lectures, and research, Dr. Isen found some time to talk with me about her findings.

Professor Isen told me her experiment scheduled active doctors at a busy hospital whenever they could spare a few minutes away from their rounds. One group was given, along with the diagnostic materials for the task, a plastic sandwich bag containing ten hard candies and tied with a piece of red yarn, and a note thanking them for their participation. This is the standard treat she uses in experiments to make people feel good or valued (in other words, to create *positive affect*, as they say in researchspeak). Professor Isen laughed as she recalled the test. "Actually, for the doctors, we did break down and put in four Hershey's Miniatures because we were afraid we needed our 'big guns.'"

The other group of doctors, the control group, received only thanks for their participation, *after* the task was completed.

The differences were striking. Isen said, "The doctors who got the candy didn't jump to conclusions. They realized quickly what the domain of the illness was, and they were correct. But they continued to check their diagnosis against new information as it came in." The doctors who received no candy were less likely to be as methodical. They had a tendency to distort information they were given or ignore facts that didn't fit with their preliminary hypotheses. Professor Isen says where positive affect was created the doctors were more willing to see what was there, less defensive about their hypotheses, and less likely to feel that they had to be right no matter what.[1]

Which doctor would you like working on your case? I asked Professor Isen if it might be a good idea to bring a bag of treats the next time I headed to the doctor's office. She begged off my question. I could understand why. Most doctors (and who knows, our own doctors might end up reading this book) would like to think they are focused and open to all the facts as they go about their work. But on the off chance—hey, it can't hurt—I think I'll bake cookies before my next checkup!

THE FEEL-GOOD EFFECT

What was it about a lousy bag of candy that made such a profound difference, anyway?

Professor Isen's hypothesis is that the good feelings generated by something as simple as a small bag of sweets and an expression of appreciation intervene in the release of dopamine. Dopamine is the chemical in the brain normally associated with happiness—the feel-good neurotransmitter. As Isen explains, dopamine is released when people are excited by a challenge or feeling good, activating the parts of the brain with dopamine receptors—mainly the frontal regions, where complex thinking and conflict resolution are headquartered. Many of Isen's other experiments have proved a conclusive link between feeling good and thinking better and/or settling disputes.

Professor Isen researches what makes people feel good. She has not specifically focused on the role Thank You Power might play in feeling good, but she is very familiar with the skepticism some might have about counting one's blessings. She says that when she started down her own research path, "it was uncharted territory. It's a hot topic now, but back then [1970], there was no one working on it. There were people who denigrated the importance of positive affect."

The proof was in the research. "When I would give a talk," she continued, "people were nice but skeptical. I had this feeling that my data were my shield. My findings were extremely strong, and no one could argue with them on a scientific basis."[2] The naysayers these days are awfully quiet.

THE UNIVERSALITY OF GRATITUDE

While the idea may seem radical to some today, the truth is since the beginning of time man has recognized the good feeling that comes from being appreciated. *Thank you* is probably the phrase you have uttered longer than any other. With the possible exception of *da-da* or some variation of the word *bottle*, thank you is one of the first things a mother coos to her infant. You rarely use da-da and ma-ma these days, but thank you still gets a workout.

The notion of gratitude is just as timeless. Gratitude is that sense of thanks one has for blessings or gifts received for which nothing is expected in return. You may want to return the favor, but it's not anticipated or required. It is thank you for those gifts in life—small or large—for which there is no quid pro quo.

The etymology of the word *gratitude* helps explain it. *Gratitude* originates from the old Latin word *gratus*—meaning *thankful, pleasing*—which has its roots in *gratia*, which means *favor, pleasing quality*, or *goodwill*. Derivatives of the Latin root can be found in a number of other languages. The Sanskrit word *grnati* means *sing praise*. In Lithuanian, *gririu* means *to praise or celebrate*. During the thirteenth century the short prayer before a meal came to be called *grace*. To take it even further, in Greek, the word for grace is *charis*, the root of the word *charisma*, a pleasing quality that you either have or you don't.[3] And if you really want to ride the word roller coaster, hang on for this: beginning with an unmerited gift (*grace*), gratitude is that pleasing quality (*charisma*) that makes one want to express appreciation or sing praise (*grnati*) even though no appreciation is expected.

The origins of the word *thank* are just as interesting. *Thank* is derived from the Old English word *pancian*, which means *to give thanks*. The root of this word, *panc*, is also the root word for the word *think*.[4] To me that speaks to what is really the essence of Thank You Power: your mind. If you don't engage the mind, concentrate, and focus on what's enhanced your life, gratitude is nonexistent.

> *No duty is more urgent than that of returning thanks.*
> —SAINT AMBROSE

Virtually every religion in the world observes some practice of giving thanks. Here's a sampling:

- *If you are thankful, surely I will increase you.*[5]
- *Rejoice always, pray without ceasing, in everything give thanks; for this is the will of God in Christ Jesus for you.*[6]
- *This is the day which the* LORD *hath made; we will rejoice and be glad in it.*[7]
- *Let us rise up and be thankful, for if we didn't learn a lot today, at least we learned a little, and if we didn't learn a little, at least we didn't get sick, and if we got sick, at least we didn't die; so, let us all be thankful.*[8] (In other words, no matter how bad things are . . . they could have been worse.)

These lines are from Jewish, Buddhist, Muslim, and Christian texts—can you guess which came from which?

Thank You Power is more than just ticking off a laundry list of all the good things in life. If that were all there were to it, you'd have a list as long as your arm without batting an eye. Eyes to see this, hands to hold it, time to spend reading it, a brain with which to think about and comprehend it, and so on. If it were just list making, getting ready for the weekly trip to the supermarket would have all of us in good shape.

In a way, gratitude is the gift that keeps on giving. First there is the gift itself: a loving gesture, a kind word, a cookie when no treats were expected—the gift itself evokes pleasure for the recipient. That's enough to give someone a bit of a glow. But the pleasure extends beyond just the gift. Unspoken in the exchange is the recognition that the recipient was worthy of this gift. A history student might be proud to earn an A thanks to hours of study. But he will be *grateful* for the teacher who spent a few minutes after class explaining a point he didn't understand.

For the people in the study who made this connection, their moods and emotions were brighter, more optimistic, more hopeful—more positive. People experiencing positive affect are more confident and energetic. They feel their lives are going well, that they are meeting the goals they've set for themselves and dealing with the challenges that come along the way. They are more outgoing. They are, in a word, *happier*.[9] Take a look at the following Gratitude Questionnaire, developed by the authors of the gratitude study you read about in chapter 1. How do *you* score on the test?

For years, experts have argued about what makes a person happy. Check out the self-help industry and you'll find at least a hundred interventions to increase happiness. Most of it is a lot of talk—common sense to some, hot air to others—but with little solid evidence to back up the platitudes. There has been only limited scientific work to determine conclusively how to achieve positive affect. In her experiments, as we mentioned earlier, Alice

The Gratitude Questionnaire (GQ-6)[10]

Using the scale below as a guide, write a number beside each statement to indicate how much you agree with it.

1 = strongly disagree
2 = disagree
3 = slightly disagree
4 = neutral
5 = slightly agree
6 = agree
7 = strongly agree

____ 1. *I have so much in life to be thankful for.*
____ 2. *If I had to list everything that I felt grateful for, it would be a very long list.*
____ 3. *When I look at the world, I see so much to be grateful for.*
____ 4. *I am grateful to a wide variety of people.*
____ 5. *As I get older I find myself more able to appreciate the people, events, and situations that have been part of my life history.*
____ 6. *Very short amounts of time can go by before I feel grateful to something or someone.*

So how'd you do? Just add up your points. The higher your score, the more grateful you are. A score of 39 or

higher means you are intensely grateful. Under 24
means you could probably use a little Thank You
Power in your life. A score of 33 means you are in the
mid-range of gratitude.

Isen gives the unsuspecting test subject a bag of candy or another
inexpensive gift, such as nail clippers or a notepad. While it
works to prime a test subject, most of us would be freaked out of
our minds if a pair of nail clippers kept landing in our mailbox
every day.

Practicing Thank You Power could also be a useful way to
achieve the positive affect that leads to happiness. And while happiness, like money, doesn't grow on trees, it *can*, like trees, be
grown, according to Chris Peterson, professor of psychology at
the University of Michigan. "The people who are grateful are living better lives," he says.

Dr. Peterson says anyone can become happy—if one wants to.
"Our research suggests you can change happiness around," he
told me. "A lot of people say
happiness is a genetic thing.
It's fixed, that it's the way you
are. You are born that way. We
aren't sure we believe that.

> *Virtue is not hereditary.*
> —THOMAS PAINE

We've known for a long time that you can 'make' someone
unhappy. That's depression. But could you make people happy?"
Peterson asked. "The answer is yes. But it's not a superficial, one-
shot deal. It's not five easy steps and you're done. It's hard work."[11]

Professor Peterson was asked by his former professor at the University of Pennsylvania, Martin Seligman, to join him in trying to find out exactly what really matters in making people feel happy. The result was a grocery list of twenty-four qualities that typify happy, satisfied people. These attributes, called *signature strengths*, seem to contribute most to an individual's fulfillment and character.

These were some of the qualifications of a signature strength:

♦ The quality must contribute to one's ability to live the *good life*, something that would pass the *deathbed test*. In other words, as you breathe your last breath, would you look back on it and be glad it was part of your life? Remember Barbara Bush's 1990 commencement address to Wellesley University graduates when she advised that you will never regret not closing one more deal in exchange for time with family?

♦ The strength must be something that is *valued on its own*.

♦ The practice of this strength must result in *positives* such as respect, satisfaction, and good health.

♦ The strength must *not diminish other people*. It can be a quality that inspires admiration but not jealousy. Beauty would not qualify as a signature strength, but patience would.

♦ The trait must be a constant in a person's life, not something that comes and goes according to mood or life events. A person might be kind in all situations, but called on to be brave only when faced by someone with a gun.

These are traits to which anyone can aspire. As Peterson and Seligman assert in their book, "All people can aspire to have strong character in a way that they cannot aspire to be good-looking or physically resilient."[12] You can check out the list of these signature strengths in the appendix, where also you'll find a link to an online test to discover your greatest strengths.

All of the character strengths are important, but Peterson says three of them—hope, love, and gratitude—kept coming back as the most *rewarding*. Hope and love can at times be challenging to cultivate. If you are a despicable human being, becoming lovable won't happen easily. If you are destitute, hope can be hard to come by unless your circumstances change. But gratitude, Peterson says, is something you can grow. "You can do it in degrees. You can do it in baby steps."

> *Choose always the way that seems the best, however rough it may be. Custom will soon render it easy and agreeable.*
> —PYTHAGORAS

For the first baby step, Peterson asked his students to each write what he called a *gratitude letter* to someone who had been especially kind to them but never properly thanked. Then they were asked to deliver their letters in person. Peterson was blown away by what happened.

"We had no idea how wildly successful it would be," the professor exclaimed. "It's positively moving! It's interesting; we've done it with college students, and they almost always thank mom or dad. The parents just go crazy. We've had parents pull us aside and say, 'This makes the tuition that I have to pay worth it!'" Peterson laughed as he related some of those conversations.

"So I guess this is a $100,000 letter for some! There is no downside."

THANK YOU POWER
Write a gratitude letter to someone.

It's probably not surprising that the parents of Peterson's students were floored by receiving the letter. Most parents would fall over in a dead faint at receiving a *written* thank you for *anything* from their child. The heartfelt sentiments expressed in these letters, acknowledging the sacrifices made for their educations, and the promise to put that education to its best use were things these parents never expected to receive. Of course the parents were happy, but the students writing the letters were happy too.

It was more than knowing that they had pleased their parents. Yes, the exchange of the letter was for the recipient a tangible acknowledgment of the value of what they had received. It was hardly a repayment of a debt; few parents expect to be reimbursed for tuition money. The students could tell how much their letters were appreciated, and they liked that. But the warm glow from exchanging the letter lasted long after the visit took place. For up to thirty days after the letters were given, the letter *writers* reported feeling elevated or happier.

Peterson and others believe it has less to do with the actual writing of the letter than with the reinforcement of the relationship between the giver and the recipient. That connection between individuals, underscored by the gratitude letter, is what scientists suspect is the key to Thank You Power. "We are not hermits; we are inherently social," Peterson explains. "What gratitude does is build bonds with other people. It makes those bonds stronger and more positive."

But the afterglow of those gratitude letters eventually faded. Despite all the time and emotion spent in choosing someone to thank, composing the letter, and the often heartwarming visit to read the letter to its recipient, the boost in self-reported happiness eventually dissipated. The good feelings disappeared. As positive as the effects of the gratitude letter were—and for roughly a month, they were nice—they were short-lived.

Looking for a longer-lasting benefit, the test subjects were asked to count their blessings daily in the manner described in chapter 1. Here, too, partici-pants wrote down three things they considered blessings in their lives and asked them-selves why each blessing had happened. There was nothing

> *Silent gratitude isn't much use to anyone.*
> —GLADYS BERTHA STERN

particularly magical about the *why* except that it made people focus during the exercise and put more thought into it.

Laziness was not allowed. The people had to write their thoughts down. Merely thinking about their blessings made it tempting to skip through the exercise. For the six months that the participants did the daily exercises, they reported noticeably higher levels of happiness. Their emotions, feelings, and outlooks were positive.[13]

Megan Mahoney didn't write a letter to the person for whom she was grateful. Instead she walked up to him and hugged him.

Her gratitude was directed toward Dan Engle, an Indiana man who would still be a total stranger if Mother Nature hadn't brought the pair together.

Megan was driving from her Missouri home to visit some college pals in Cincinnati. The weather was perfect, and she was eager for the quiet time in the car. Her mother had been recently diagnosed with breast cancer, and the strain of her illness was weighing on Megan. Megan stopped for something to eat around Terre Haute, Indiana, when the weather turned. Mild rain at first, suddenly the heavens opened and the water came down in torrents. Megan had just decided to pull over to the side of the road and wait out the rain when something hit her car. "I heard metal and debris slamming against the right side of my car," she told me. "Then I heard glass breaking."

Megan slammed on the brakes, but it felt as though someone was pushing her car. "I remember thinking, *This is how I'm going to die*. It's weird though. I wasn't upset. I wasn't freaking out: 'Oh gosh! I'm going to die!' I was just very accepting and peaceful." Then the SUV flipped over. Megan hit her head and was knocked unconscious. The next thing Megan knew, she was in Dan Engle's house. "I remember waking up, and I was in this man's house, on his couch, with a blanket on me," she says.

Turns out, Megan's car was hit by a tornado. Despite wearing her seat belt, Megan was literally sucked out of the sunroof window and thrown about three hundred yards from where her car landed. Police say the vehicle probably cartwheeled end over end a dozen times before it landed. Her safety belt was still fastened.

Engle, who lived nearby, had ventured out after the storm to survey the damage. He found Megan, dazed, wandering through a nearby field. Because debris blocked all the roads in the area, it was difficult for ambulances to get through. So he took Megan home and put her in his vehicle and drove her to the hospital himself. Bruised and bloody, incredibly Megan suffered no broken bones. Her midsection was black and blue where the seat belt had dug into her. She also had a concussion and some pretty nasty cuts, including one just millimeters from a main vein on her right arm. But it could have been much worse. She was very, very lucky.

Megan remembers a saying her family has: "If your mother passes away, something good will happen to you." Megan's grand-mother had died the summer before. Since her death, Megan's mom had been diagnosed with breast cancer. The family had begun to wonder if maybe that good thing wasn't going to happen after all.

Once Megan reached the hospital and got settled, she asked someone what day it was. It was March 31: her late grandmother's birthday. Megan says, "I got my good thing." By all accounts, Megan should have been dead and she wasn't. She and her rela-tives now think there may actually be some truth to that old fam-ily adage after all.

A couple months after the accident, Megan went back to Indiana with tears in her eyes to thank Dan Engle—the Good Samaritan—for his deed. Engle was thrilled to see Megan doing so well. "I am so grateful to be alive and to be here," Megan says. "I feel like I have been saved for a reason. Maybe to take care of my mom? But it was a miracle. It scares me to think that it was a mir-acle. But they do happen in real life."[14]

You may be persuaded by now that Thank You Power, regu-larly tallying up the good things in life, is a "good thing" in itself. So . . . ?

THE DOMINO EFFECT

—

Feeling good sets in motion a series of tumblers that unlock some amazing doors, all of them beginning with that positive state to which Dr. Isen has dedicated her professional career to understanding. The bottom line of her studies is this: People who feel positively think differently. They think *better.*

In one study, people at a mall were made to feel happy by giving them a small gift. Later, in what the shoppers thought was an unrelated survey, those same people said their cars and televisions performed better as compared to the responses of a control group who received nothing.

Feeling good also helps you think more creatively, making associations that you wouldn't necessarily make in a neutral frame of mind. You also become better at problem solving. After inducing happiness with a gift, test subjects were given seemingly unrelated words. Those who'd gotten small gifts were better at making associations between the words than the empty-handed control group.

Here's an example:

1. What one word links these three words together?
Cottage   Blue   Mouse

Here's another one to try:

2. What one word links these three words together?
Atomic   Mower   Foreign

Once you are given the answers (see * below), it's easy to make the connection. People who feel good make those associations faster.

*1. Cheese 2. Power

In another one of Dr. Isen's experiments, the test subjects were randomly given one of two films to watch. One was neutral, designed to evoke no emotion. The other movie was mildly funny and had viewers laughing. After the films, subjects were assigned the task of attaching a candle to a bulletin board so it could be lit. They were given the candle, a book of matches, and a box of tacks. Trouble was, the tacks were too short and the candle too breakable to nail directly to the wall. How would *you* handle this dilemma?

The answer is to dump the tacks, use the box as a candleholder, and then pin the box to the wall. Only 20 percent of the people who saw the neutral film figured this out within ten minutes. But the people who saw the funny film *did* figure it out: 58 percent had the candle mounted and lit within ten minutes in one survey; 75 percent got it right that quickly in another.

The happy people were better able to engage their imaginations, less constrained by assumptions. They were flexible in their thinking, perceiving unusual but sensible ways of categorizing material and relationships between categories that at first glance might seem unrelated, like the word groups just mentioned.

Isen has also found that positive emotions make people more helpful to others. And since helping someone else makes people feel good about what they've done, the positive feelings continue and even amplify, creating more good feelings.[15]

There is even good evidence that focusing on a singular happy moment can help kids perform better at school. A group of four-year-olds were asked to think of two events, one that "made you feel so happy that you just wanted to jump up and down" and another that "made you just sit and smile." The control group focused on a nonemotional event. The kids thought about this event for thirty seconds and then were given a test that required learning a task. Those children who had the happy memory did it better and faster. Another study found that kids who focused for less than a minute on a happy event before a test performed better.[16]

What positive feelings *won't* do is give you a bum steer. While feeling good makes the world around you seem better, it doesn't make it seem better than it really is. Isen and other researchers have discovered that when everything else is equal, people who are in positive-feeling states rate other people more positively and perceive relatively neutral or only somewhat-positive consumer products more positively. It won't make you appreciate something *not* appreciable.

In the experiment that confirmed this, Dr. Isen again gave one group of participants a small gift that made them feel good. The control group, as usual, got nothing though at the conclusion of the experiment, they were thanked for participating. Then both groups were shown neutral, positive, and negative pictures. It could have been a pile of sticks for the neutral picture, a fuzzy puppy for a positive one, and a homeless person from the Depression as a negative picture. The group that had gotten the gift evaluated the neutral and positive images as "better" but not the negative material.

"It's not like rose-colored glasses," Dr. Isen said. "Pictures of Hitler and the reign of the Third Reich would not suddenly seem OK if you were in a positive state brought on by a fifty-cent gift. Positive affect does not make everything seem better. It makes only those things with the *potential* to become better seem better because of the active process of seeing the positive aspects of the thing. "It is not," she concludes, "just being off in your own world, saying 'everything is OK.' You won't lose all judgment."[17]

That last point is important. People who feel good don't become Pollyannas or patsies. Though they may be more inclined to help others, they will only help those who deserve it. If a person or cause is disliked or unlikable, Isen's studies found that people who feel good not only won't help, but they are also less likely than other groups to be *pushed* into helping.

What people with Thank You Power *will* do is inspire those around them to do well. If a leader ranks high on positive emotion, his team will probably perform better.[18] Salespeople are more helpful to their customers, more flexible, and more respectful.[19] So make it a point—today—to make people in your world feel *good*. Say thank you to someone you may have taken for granted—the security guard at your office building or your child's teacher. Perhaps bring lemonade to the gardener working in the yard. Just because someone is paid to perform a service doesn't mean a thank you shouldn't come his way.

THANK YOU POWER
Say thank you to someone overdue to hear it.

three

Don't Sweat the Small Stuff—
Notice It!

IT'S QUIET ON THE SERENGETI. INCREDIBLY QUIET. ON one of the most famous wildlife refuges on earth, one hears nothing. The wheat-colored landscape stretches as far as the eye can see. Solitary acacia trees occasionally dot the landscape like mile markers—a testament to just how great the distances are. A ten-minute drive brings us to the faraway tree, only to see the next is just as far off—like a desert mirage, only real. The thin, black line ahead on the horizon will soon reveal itself to be thousands and thousands of snorting, grunting wildebeests, part of the annual migration of 1.5 million that travel these plains.

Here, though, it is totally silent. Or is it? We sit in the Land Cruiser, engine extinguished, staring at a horizon that blurs into the haze of the sky. The smallest of sounds is amplified. The clank of cooling parts under the hood. The gurgle of someone's stomach digesting food. We wait and we watch. And . . . we wonder: Have we come ten thousand miles to animal watch at a place where there is not one single living thing?

But wait. A noise overhead proves to be the flapping wings of a vulture surveying the landscape. The rustle to our right is a young gazelle, blending unnoticed into the brush. That empty patch of grass over to the left is, in fact, home to a herd of topi, grazing aimlessly. I look down at the ground: some kind of beetle is industriously running to and fro as part of his species' life dance.

There are scores of creatures here, I realize. I am simply too deeply entrenched in my do-it-now, fly-through-life mode to notice. I take a deep breath and settle into my seat, binoculars in hand. "*Simba*, eleven o'clock," our guide says in a calm voice. *Simba*, Swahili for *lion*. Five sets of field glasses turn in unison. There she is: the lioness we had hoped to see this day. So much for empty fields.

THANK YOU POWER
*Focus on something of beauty, and
share it with someone else.*

There is something utterly magical about the out-of-doors. Whether you live in the city or the Serengeti, the rejuvenating properties of nature are awesome. You'll learn more about just *how* awesome in the next chapter. Focus on a single flower. Marvel at the intricacies of the veins of a leaf. Observe the myriad of colors as sunlight glints on the hair of a pet. You could go to Africa to do it—or simply step out of your door.

Our family vacation to Africa was the realization of a lifelong dream of mine. The lessons I learned there, I hope to practice for the rest of my life. The calm that comes from hearing the wind speak. The universality of nurturing: mother elephants are just as protective of their young as I am. The thrill of seeing the sun fall off the horizon. Perhaps the most important lesson of all was learned there on the Serengeti Plain: *there is magic in each moment.*

There *is* magic in each moment. Thank You Power—with its emphasis on the blessings found in the mundane, everyday miracles —helps you find that magic. But you won't see it if you are barreling through life. I was reminded of that by my little girl in, of all places, LaGuardia Airport.

We'd just landed—finally—on a much-delayed return flight from a family vacation with relatives in Georgia. I was blasting through the entrance to baggage claim, determined to find our stuff and get away from anyone and everything that has to do with air travel.

"Mommy, look at the kitty," my daughter, Mikaela, exclaimed as she trotted to keep up with me.

"Yes, honey, it's very nice," I replied mindlessly, not breaking stride. From my peripheral vision, I saw a couple of adults possibly holding something. It could have been a sack of potatoes, for all I knew, 'cause I wasn't about to stop.

"Mom, isn't it neat?" My child had no idea she was being completely tuned out.

"Yes, it's *amazing*!" I still had not seen a cat. Seen one, seen 'em all. We've got one named Fluffy at home. I bet Airport Cat looks just like her.

We collected our bags, dragged them to the car, and headed home. No further comment about Airport Cat.

The next day at work, I was sitting in the newsroom, writing the script for *Inside Edition*, when one of my colleagues came up with some visitors.

"Deborah, I want you to meet . . ." I stood and turned to greet . . . Airport Cat! Yup, that sack of potatoes and the couple who'd been holding her were right there in our newsroom. Scottie and Rodney Colvin and their cat, Piper, were enjoying their fifteen minutes of national fame. Piper was the gigantic cat that had gotten herself stuck in the South Carolina family's tree for eight days. When Piper finally hurled herself eighty feet to freedom, it was a story, because the home video camera was rolling as she parachuted herself to safety.

> *Happiness shared is happiness doubled.*
> —SWEDISH PROVERB

I could see why my daughter noticed Airport Cat. It was one of the biggest cats I'd ever seen. Mikaela saw Piper simply because she still has those naturally wide-open eyes, eager to see everything. I strive for it, but despite my best efforts, I still am too often so focused on the business of life that I miss the magic moments along the way. That night, I said thank you for the reminder from my little girl and that big cat that everyday enchantment can be found in the most ordinary of places.

An awareness of the mundane is what struck Whitney Toombs when she started her daily practice of Thank You Power. "I don't think I ever quite noticed the street players before," she says of her daily commute on the New York City subway. "Lately I've not only noticed that they're there on the subway platform; they're actually good! Yesterday there was this incredible man with a violin, playing this wonderful Bach piece."

Just out of college and enjoying her first job in the Big Apple, Whitney finds something every day that delights her about her new city. But she never expected the daily trip through New York's grimy and often unpredictable subway system to be one of them. Now she walks expectantly down the subway steps, curious to see what musical delights (or disasters!) will greet her this time. She says Thank You Power opened her eyes to it.

"I think what this did for me was help me go back through every part of my day. Obviously what happened at work and what you did at night with your friends are easy to remember. But I don't think I'd have paid much attention to my trip to work if I hadn't done this. Who'd have thought *that* would have been anything you'd later be grateful for?" she says with a laugh.[1]

That's Thank You Power: giving you gifts when you least expect it.

Sixth-grade teacher Neal Feldman doesn't expect those kinds of gifts when he's at his job, but he's realized that they happen pretty often. He recalls one moment with one of his students, about six weeks into the school year.

"All of a sudden, right in the middle of my lesson, this boy in my class raises his arms over his head and in a very loud voice says, 'I *love* my life!' It was the darnedest thing," Feldman said, laughing. "Just, *boom*! Right in the middle of class, he burst out.

Then the next second, he was right back there, focusing with the rest of the class. I've never seen anything like it."

Ordinarily, there's a penalty for talking out in class. But Feldman couldn't bring himself to issue it. "I figured he's feeling pretty good, and he's in my class when he's feeling it," he explained. "I just took it as a compliment." Feldman also took the trouble to call the boy's mother, to pass along the amusing moment.[2]

It's rare that a parent gets that kind of affirmation that his child is truly happy. The teacher's story must have brought a smile to that mom's face and given her a lift for the rest of the day. No doubt that night, her son's classroom outburst was one of the moments for which she said thank you. The pass-along impact of Thank You Power is pretty strong.

THANK YOU POWER
*List three mundane things
that enhance your daily life.*

Ann Rubenstein Tisch probably would have seen that heroic cat because she doesn't miss those kinds of moments. Whether it's pointing out a beautiful tree during an afternoon drive or relishing the prospect of the storm promised by some menacing clouds, she is tuned in to the little things. Maybe that's why she's accomplished so much in her life.

The work she did as a correspondent for NBC News would have been accomplishment enough for most people. From her base in Chicago and later New York, Ann became known for hard-hitting stories that always emphasized the humanity of the people caught up in news events. It was a single moment during one of those stories that led to the latest chapter in her life.

"I was doing a story for *Nightly News*," Ann recalled over breakfast. "It was on an inner-city school that opened a day care center for its teen moms so they could come back and finish school while their babies were being cared for down the hall. It was a noble effort." Or so everyone thought. Ann's epiphany came while interviewing some of the teenagers who were taking advantage of the day care program.

"I asked one of the girls—she was just the size of a minute—I said, 'Where do you see yourself in five years?' And she just started weeping." Ann's voice revealed the astonishment she felt at the time. "And a lightbulb went off, and I remember at that very moment thinking, *Oh my gosh! I don't think we're doing enough for these kids. She knows she's stuck!*"

Ann filed her story, but the tiny young mother haunted her thoughts. "I remember thinking about it later that night. The idea is to offer these girls a completely different path. The day care center was noble. The people who put it together were amazing. But that wasn't the answer. They were still stuck."

Ann was stuck too—stuck on the idea that girls in the inner city deserved better. Over time, she became convinced that as hard as she worked as a journalist, there was a different job she had to do that would have more impact and longer-lasting implications than an evening news story. She put away her reporter's pen and paper, gave birth to two daughters, and shortly after that, also gave birth to a radical idea in public education: she founded an inner-city public girls' school, operated with the same rigorous standards as New York City's top private girls' schools.

The Young Women's Leadership School (TYWLS) opened its doors in Harlem in 1996. It offers inner-city girls a college-preparatory program with an emphasis on the future. No matter how bad a girl's life might be today, TYWLS gives her a chance to work for a happier future. According to Ann, you can't overstate how difficult some girls' lives are: broken homes, abusive families, economic despair. "Some of them haven't eaten dinner the night before," she said, punching the tabletop for emphasis. "But they come to school in a full uniform and their homework neatly done."

The school sees itself as an oasis of calm in a turbulent outside world. "What we say to our girls every morning is 'Whatever is going on in your life, your parents are screwed up, whatever—it's not your fault. For the eight hours you are with us, just forget it. This is about you. There's an opportunity for you here. You don't have to live that way, so work forward.'" The school has guidance counselors and psychologists along with the teaching staff to help the girls achieve their success.

It's working: every single graduate of The Young Women's Leadership School has gone on to attend a four-year college or university. Nearly nine out of ten of those have gotten their degrees. Ann believes the reason for the girls' success is actually quite simple: it's expected of them. "My mother used to say if nothing is expected of you, then nothing is what you'll do." Ann continued, "For years and years in our crummy, rundown schools, people said, 'You can't expect anything from these kids. Look at their home lives, and look at that.' So they expect nothing, and they do nothing. I don't like to say they are defying the odds because that's a bit negative. I like to say that they are changing expectations."

Those changes in expectations are pretty widespread. Before TYWLS could open its doors, the New York Civil Liberties Union went to court, claiming it was discriminatory. Others said it was "demeaning" to assume that girls could be better taught in classes without boys. Ann said that in a weird way, the critics were a blessing. "They made so much noise and focused so much attention on our school that we became the subject of front-page news, cocktail chatter, and dinner-party conversations. How thankful I was when the effect of our critics and the controversy forced the issue of public education to the forefront! It got people interested, engaged, and talking about us."[3]

Indeed it did. The school was called a "bold gamble" by the *Washington Post*.[4] The complaint was dismissed, and the idea caught on. There are now seven TYWLS operating around the country.

Not bad for a woman who still refers to herself as "just a kid from Kansas." Ann's life is vastly different from the lives of the kids who went to high school with her. Thank You Power played a big role in making it happen. Whether it was the big-time TV job or the solid marriage or the two healthy, energetic daughters, Ann has always acknowledged her blessings and been careful to give credit where it's due. She's raising her daughters to do the same. Very little is allowed to intrude on the family's weekly religious observances when the children and their parents give thanks.

But none of this explains why Ann Tisch chose such a daunting way to express her gratitude. "This may sound corny, but for lack of a better word, it's about humanity. It's about giving back," she explained. "I don't think anything can make someone feel better than that. I think there is just no substitute feeling, and I am grateful for the opportunity to do it." She continued, "I feel so blessed and so grateful that, as a parent, I am able to choose the type of education my own children have, coed, all-girls, public, or private. When you know you are that blessed, you also know there is an enormous other side. My gratitude led me to make things better for those hundreds of inner-city girls. Knowing what education did for me and being thankful for it, led me to want to make sure others had the same chance . . . or at least a shot at what I had."[5]

As of this writing, seven hundred girls have graduated from the The Young Women's Leadership Schools. Think of the opportunities they have now that all started with one moment. One moment. One struggling young mom. And one woman who never forgot her.

A GRATEFUL HEART IS ALWAYS READY FOR A MIRACLE

Aron Ralston is acutely aware of the power of gratitude. He's the mountain climber whose fall in a Utah canyon left him trapped with his arm caught under a boulder. Alone, running low on water, and after five days, suffering from dehydration and hypothermia, he did the unthinkable to free himself. We crossed paths in 2004 when he was on tour, promoting his book, *Between a Rock and a Hard Place.*

He told me that the answer to his predicament came to him in a vision, a vision that helped him believe he had a future. "It sounds kind of odd, but I left my body and walked through the canyon wall. A panel door opened, closed behind me, and I'm in a living room. A little boy—a three-year-old wearing a red polo shirt, playing with his trucks on a sunlit floor—turns to me and looks up and says, 'Daddy,' and comes running across. And I scoop him up and put him on my shoulder."

In the vision, as Aron was scooping up the little boy, he saw that one of his arms had been amputated. It was a sign to Aron that he *would* last through his ordeal. It was also a sign that to do so he would have to perform a crude form of surgery on his right arm. He'd considered that option the first day he was trapped. Thanks to that vision, he did it. First he broke the bones of his arm, fashioned a tourniquet, and then amputated his dying arm with the knife from his backpack.

One can't help but cringe at the thought. I know I visibly did as I interviewed Aron on national television. But as Aron described the moment to me, his face was filled with light. He recalled the moment of amputation as a rebirth, a birth that *this* time around he fully understands. Aron is acutely aware that his life today is a gift, one for which he is grateful each day.

"I think what I carry is the gratitude toward the universe that I'm alive and here. I try day to day to experience life with a fraction of the euphoria I felt in that moment when I had my life back."

For Ralston, his Thank You Power has a focus: the wilderness where he very nearly lost his life and found it again. He is still climbing and trying to work for wilderness preservation. "I owe a great deal to the wilderness. It gave me this experience, and if people feel inspired from this story, it's because the wilderness was there to provide it."[6]

THE POWER OF A THOUGHT

I read once that the average person has something like sixty thousand thoughts a day. I was, of course, immediately skeptical about this, wondering, *How do they come up with this figure?* Did they hog-tie some unwitting volunteer and make him sit with electrodes on his skull all day? Who did the counting? Did the volunteer make little tally marks, or was he sharing each thought with an even sadder soul who was forced to sit with the thinker/volunteer? I doubt very much if anyone knows how many thoughts a person has in a day. But let's say for the sake of argument that we do have thousands and thousands of disparate thoughts and ideas flashing through our consciousness. How many of your thoughts are rooted in gratitude?

Donna Davis tries to make sure at least some of hers are, every day. A travel agent outside Philadelphia, Donna says that Thank You Power has helped her do great things in a real-people, real-life kind of way.

Donna describes herself as the quieter of the two Davis sisters. A chatty, engaging woman with a ready smile, it's hard to believe she's the quiet one. Donna and her sister, Diane, are cochairs of Philadelphia's Susan G. Komen Breast Cancer Race for the Cure. Donna says she hates public speaking. She must be good at hiding it because the first year the Davis women chaired the race, they raised over $2 million for breast cancer research and education.

Donna credits the nightly conversations or thoughts she has when she goes to bed. "I reflect on the day, I think about what's coming up the next day. I ask for guidance. And I am thanking my angels for little things. I am also focusing on gratitude," she says.

"I look at what I've got, and I ask, 'What is coming next? Where am I in what I need to do?'"

Donna's way of living might best be described as *thankfully expectant*. Before what she considers blessings have even come, she's already thankful for them—and somehow minimiracles just seem to happen!

Her sister was looking to buy a new house and spotted a charming home in a cute neighborhood. Only problem was, it wasn't for sale. One week later, the women left on a trip out of town, still thinking about their dream house. Wouldn't you know? When they returned home, the house had just gone on sale. Diane Davis lives there now.

Donna says her involvement with the breast cancer charity came about in much the same way. Someone asked if she wanted to run in the Race for the Cure. She replied, "I'm not athletic!" Told that it wasn't a running race-to-the-finish-line, she thought it might be a nice way to honor the people in her life who'd dealt with breast cancer. It was all in keeping with a woman who has served as a music therapist for autistic children, hugged hospitalized HIV/AIDS babies, and worked with teens in a hospital psychiatric ward. Says Donna, "People just want to feel loved."[7] Donna says it makes her feel good to give a bit of herself to others.

THANK YOU POWER
What's not *necessary?*

Donna Davis may have felt led by Thank You Power to do something extraordinary, like raise millions to fight breast cancer. Attorney Philip Hilder did something just as monumental, at least to his family, it is: he put away his BlackBerry.

You've probably seen Hilder on television. He's the prominent Houston attorney who represented Sherron Watkins, the whistle-blower in the famed Enron case. Always up for an intellectual challenge, Hilder agreed to test-drive Thank You Power. In the midst of flying around the country, meeting clients, preparing cases, and arguing legal briefs, the former federal prosecutor spent a few minutes each day zeroing in on just three things for which he felt thankful, as outlined in chapter 1. You may be surprised to hear that nowhere on his list will you find a big courtroom victory or a witness withering under his cross-examination. His is a list of little things.

"You are always grateful for your family," he said from O'Hare Airport, where he was waiting to catch a flight. "But doing the exercise makes you realize a lot of things happen every day that you are thankful for, that you just take for granted. You just don't usually pay attention to them."

"Such as . . . ?" I probed.

"You might be thankful for the people in your office, for the people who help you out, the ones who assist you with the children. You are thankful that the paper is there on time in the morning, the technology that makes your life easier," he ticked off. "These are matters in the day-to-day pursuit that you don't focus on, but when you stop to think, these are things that you are really appreciative of. These are the things that really make a difference in your life."[8]

Because Thank You Power puts one's focus on the seemingly mundane, many people have a tendency to discount it, according to Philip Watkins, professor of psychology at Eastern Washington State University. "They are faithful blessings. Because they are consistent, we as humans tend to not notice them. So our faithful, constant blessings we start taking for granted, and I would argue that they are some of the most important. I think the really grateful recognizes those simple pleasures and consistently takes stock of those kinds of things."[9]

It's made a difference for Philip Hilder. "I realized that part of what I am thankful for is also what I am *not* thankful for. What I am *not* thankful for is that I am always accessible, whether on the cell phone or the BlackBerry going off. People will fax a message to me at any time and want an instantaneous response. So where technology helps me stay in touch, it also has a limiting effect. It accelerates my life, and for that I am not appreciative. We live on a very fast track, which I am not sure is healthy for us. It makes me think of the simpler times of life."

So Mr. Hilder did what some in his profession would call the unthinkable. He made a firm decision to leave his BlackBerry tucked safely in its charging cradle. Most days you won't find it in his pocket unless he's on an out-of-town business trip or away from the office for an extended period. Thank You Power was behind the move.

"The exercise made me think of how connected I was, and I didn't want to be." The attorney says he realized he was disconnecting from his most important clients: his wife and four children. "With the BlackBerry, I was always checking for messages and e-mailing when I should have been devoting time to them. I want to be able to appreciate time with them. I feel like now I am just much more in tune with the family."

His clients don't seem to have noticed, and frankly, Hilder's not sure his family has either. But he has. "I like it. I do. It makes me reflect, stop, and think about the goodness around me."[10]

With three-year-old twins, a five-year-old, and an eight-year-old, there's a lot of goodness around him. Attorney Philip Hilder might make a motion that Thank You Power has reminded him to enjoy it.

four

Accentuate the Positive

*Cheerfulness is the best promoter of health,
and is as friendly to the mind as to the body.*

—JOSEPH ADDISON

IT WAS A PERFECT DAY FOR A BIKE RIDE. ANNE HJELLE left her home after lunch, excited that the weather was so ideal for her planned afternoon of mountain biking with her best friend, Debi Nicholls. They met in the parking lot at the foothills of the park where they'd spent countless hours pedaling away. It would be a tough, strenuous ride, and both women were ready. CamelBaks filled with water, helmets buckled on, and they were off.

Thirty minutes into their ride, the fun was just beginning as the terrain started to take shape. The road was rugged with all the twists and hills that make mountain bicycling an adventure.

Anne was in the lead. "I rounded a corner and saw a bike pulled over to the side. I remember thinking that was odd. Where was the rider? No one would leave their bike like that on the trail. But I didn't have time to stop and investigate. We were probably going fifteen, twenty miles an hour at that point."

It was only in retrospect that Anne recalled the abandoned bike. The next instant, as she rounded a curve past the abandoned bike, she saw a tawny flash. In a single motion, Anne was slammed onto the ground and dragged into the brush. Without making a sound, a mountain lion had pounced from out of nowhere and had now buried its jaws in her neck.

"I don't even remember hitting the ground," she told me. "It was that fast. The only thing I remember saying was calling out, 'Jesus, help me!' The other thing I remember very clearly is the mountain lion's power. It was unreal. It felt like ten guys attacking me at once. He had me by the back of the neck first; then I felt him grab on to the side of my face. He pulled and tore away the side of my face." Anne is incredibly matter-of-fact as she describes those first seconds of terror. "I didn't feel pain at the time. But I felt the strength of it." In that initial lunge, the mountain lion ripped one side of her face open like a sardine can, all the way to her eyeball.[1]

Debi had heard Anne scream. By the time she rounded the bend, Anne was at least thirty feet into the brush, being dragged toward the ravine.

Debi screamed at the beast. She picked up her bike and hurled it at the cat. It didn't flinch. Then Debi, a mother of four, hurled *herself* at the pair, grabbing Anne by the leg and trying desperately to stop the animal from taking her friend.

"I said, 'You're *not* going to do this!'" Debi recalled. "I just couldn't let him take her. I knew what would happen." Debi screamed for help as she held on to Anne's leg, hoping other riders would hear the commotion.[2]

Anne was trying furiously to beat off the creature, but to no avail. In fact, she was acutely aware of how methodically the mountain lion was altering its jaws to snap in the right spot.

"His goal, as it would be with any type of prey, was to break my neck and paralyze me," Anne explained. "He had me by the face, and I could sense that he was trying to get to my throat." With each step the lion took toward the brush, he changed his grip to get closer to Anne's windpipe.

Anne is a woman with a deep faith in Christ, and she was praying desperately for God's help. Anne fought hard, but she could not escape the lion, which was now dragging both women through the brush. The encounter lasted no more than a few minutes, during which Anne says she could feel herself fading.

The lion clamped down. Anne's airway was blocked. Her body went limp.

"I knew there was nothing I could do," she says of that moment when she could feel herself beginning to slip from consciousness. "It really was all in God's hands, and I was at peace with dying. I was trying to say good-bye to Debi, and looking into her eyes, I could see the fear. Watching it was pretty tough."

As if sent from heaven, a trio of guys on bikes arrived and immediately started hurling rocks at the lion. Just as Anne passed out, one of the rocks hit its mark: the back of the cat's neck. The killer released its grip, and Anne was saved.

As they waited deep in the brush, someone put a T-shirt on Anne's face. When the paramedics finally made their way in, one of them was shaking. Debi didn't know if it was from looking at Anne or because the lion was lurking nearby. It was dark now, and they could see its eyes reflecting back the light from flashlights. The beast was no more than thirty feet away.[3]

Anne was airlifted out of the ravine and taken to the local trauma center where surgeons painstakingly reattached her face in a six-hour operation—the first of many. When she came out of surgery, she was told that the abandoned bike she'd passed on the trail had belonged to Mark Reynolds. He had been killed by the same lion just minutes before Anne's attack. That she didn't become the lion's second meal of the day is just one of many miracles. You'll hear about some other miracles in chapter 10.

But first, the more immediate miracle: she survived. Anne Hjelle and Debi Nicholls may be strong on mountain *bikes*, but they are no match for mountain *lions*. Somehow Anne managed to keep the beast from making a fatal bite. Her face was peeled back from her skull. Puncture wounds were just millimeters from her jugular vein. How did she survive? Somehow Debi found the athleticism to leap to where her friend was being dragged. From somewhere, she found the strength to hold on and dig her heels in enough to slow the cat down. How?

Experts will tell you that the women instinctively reverted to man's primeval roots. All of their body systems were concentrated on one thing: resisting the cougar. Adrenaline pumping to give Debi superhuman strength. Instinctive presence of mind to angle Anne's neck away from the cat's jaws. Every sensor in each woman's body was channeled toward a single goal: survival.

When I interviewed Anne about her incredible story, I asked, "Did the mountain lion smell?" I had a mental (and olfactory) image of being overwhelmed by the stench of this creature. He'd already eaten one biker, and with Anne in his clutches, he clearly had intentions of a second course.

"I don't know," she told me. "I don't remember smelling anything at all."[4] She also recalled no pain (although others on the trail heard her moaning, so the pain must have been excruciating).

That's not surprising. In moments of extreme stress, the body's focus narrows, concentrating all of its attention and body systems on the stressor. Every critical aspect of the human machine is primed to run, leap, swim—whatever is necessary to survive. Noncritical functions are reduced to the point of dormancy. The senses of hearing, smell, and touch—the sensation of pain—were unnecessary for survival, so they took a backseat to the strengths Anne and her friend needed to fight the feline. Anne Hjelle is alive today because of superhuman power and her intuitive knowledge of the cat's intention, which came from a place deep inside. Anne would argue that it came from the man upstairs. She gives God all the credit for her survival.

The rest of us have the same hormones that helped Anne in her fight. In our hunter-gatherer days, man was frequently under attack. A quick rush of adrenaline, elevated heart rate, increased blood pressure, and cortisol-induced speed were often the only things that kept early man from becoming the appetizer for a bloodthirsty carnivore. The fight-or-flight response gave man the ability to outrun, outmaneuver, and outwit a predator, determining his survival.

These days the associated hormones don't get used in the same way. Our fight-or-flight hormones start flowing when we realize we've double booked ourselves for lunch. We get flustered when we realize we forgot that today is our spouse's birthday. We pull our hair out when our kids won't stop asking questions or constantly interrupt us when we are talking.

Think of how you react when you're angry. Your heart races; your pulse quickens; you become agitated and pound the table or tap your feet. All you see in your mind's eye is that jerk who ticked you off. Try as you might, that creep is stuck in your memory bank. From deep within comes the urge to attack.

The adrenaline and cortisol to launch the attack are there, but with no physical release, the stress hormones have nothing to do but wreak havoc on your digestive system, your sleep patterns, and your cardiovascular system, resulting in heart disease, just to begin the list.

THE POWER TO DE-STRESS

What if you could play out the stress scenario in *rewind*? Instead of the mind and body functions narrowing for attack, might it be possible to broaden them with the polar opposite? What if you replaced the anger with appreciation, frustration with gratitude, and pressure with tranquillity? Would the human body react in opposite fashion?

That's what Barbara Fredrickson has been trying to figure out for more than a decade. This professor of psychology, now at the University of North Carolina, has come up with what she calls the *broaden-and-build theory*. Unlike the negative emotions of anger and stress, during which the body gets prepared for immediate action, positive emotions appear to hang around for a long time. Alice Isen has proved at Cornell that feeling good has positive side effects such as better thinking, smarter negotiating, and quicker problem solving. Could feeling good also dismantle some of the stress that comes from feeling bad? Fredrickson set off to find out.

There's an old saying attributed to Winston Churchill: There are three things that terrify any man: trying to climb a building that's leaning toward you, trying to kiss a woman who's leaning away from you, and . . . giving a speech in public.

Fredrickson and her team went for the speech. Using students from the University of Michigan as test subjects (each being paid thirty dollars to participate), the team invited them into a room in which a camera and video monitor were situated. The kids were told that they had one minute to prepare a three-minute speech on a to-be-determined topic. They were also told that their speeches would be videotaped and possibly later evaluated by their peers for a portion of their grades. The students were monitored for blood pressure, heart rate, and other signs of stress, which each participant clearly exhibited. Understandably, they were nervous about the critical speech they had just learned they had to deliver.

Fredrickson and her team prepared four random short films. One movie, "Puppy," showed a cute puppy waddling and playing with a flower, eliciting amusement. "Waves" evoked contentment, with scenes of ocean waves breaking on a beach. The third, "Cry," featured a boy crying as he watches his father die. The fourth was "Sticks," a neutral film featuring an old computer screen saver of sticks piling up that elicited no emotion whatsoever. The students were randomly assigned one of four movies to watch.

As it turned out, no one actually had to give a speech, but everyone was stressed-out at the prospect of it. However, the people who saw the positive films de-stressed faster. Seeing happy and pleasant images on film *undid* the physical effects of stress, measurably so. The physical signs of stress—elevated blood pressure, faster heart and breathing rates—that were exhibited by all the students, upon hearing of the proposed impromptu speech, disappeared faster for the students who saw the positive images.[5]

Dr. Fredrickson explains, "Negative emotions cause this narrowing of attention, prompting you to feel, *Oh, I want to run away.* Your body is responding by redirecting blood to the large muscles so you can run. But negative emotions have to be undone when they are no longer relevant, when you no longer feel like you are in mortal danger. Positive emotion can have this effect."[6]

Could something as simple as a funny picture truly lessen stress? Experts say it's obviously not the picture itself but the emotional memories it triggers that are the key. Thank You Power and the positive emotions it evokes may open or broaden—to use Dr. Fredrickson's word—the passageway to retrieving those positive memories more effectively.[7] Ever try to reach something stuck in a hole, but your hand is just a bit too big to fit through easily? How much simpler it would be to retrieve the object if that hole was just an inch wider. Thank You Power helps open the doorway, making it easier to draw strength from the many positive, life-affirming experiences you have had—thus interrupting the hold negative stress momentarily might have on you.

"A lot of times, the things that we experience as stressful are ongoing properties of life. But, we have this physical stress response that is meant to be temporary, and it's not." Fredrickson says exercises to create positive emotions help break the cycle: "Rituals like counting blessings or things like that give a temporary interruption that maybe allows the stress system to turn off and on the way it should."[8]

But it's like polishing your nails. If you want them to always look good, you have to keep up with it. Visit the manicurist once and you'll look great for a week. But if you fail to make a return visit, your hands will soon look pretty grim. "Writing a gratitude letter or jotting down what you're grateful for might make you feel good for a day or a week. But if you don't keep up with it, your outlook can become dark," Fredrickson says. "If you try it on for size for one month and you notice good changes, you can't assume those are permanent changes. It takes intentional effort. It needs to be sort of woven into your daily habits and daily ways."[9]

Once it is a habit, it's like putting on a Kevlar coat of armor. Thank You Power can protect you from the forces and people who would bring you down. Fredrickson has also done research to demonstrate other ways positive emotions brought on by Thank You Power can make you better.

Again she resorted to video to put her test subjects in various states of mind. This time she used five different film clips. First came "Penguins," which showed the feathery friends waddling and swimming, prompting amusement among the viewers. "Nature" was a minute-and-a-half film of fields, streams, and mountains on a beautiful, sunny day, eliciting serenity. "Witness" was a clip from the feature film of the same title and showed a bunch of Amish being taunted by passers-by. People reacted with anger and disgust to this clip. "Cliffhanger" was nearly three minutes of coverage of a mountain-climbing accident, provoking anxiety and fear. The last clip was "Sticks," a bunch of colored sticks being piled up and eliciting virtually no emotion.

After seeing one of five random films, participants in this second experiment were asked to state, in a word or two, the emotion most strongly evoked while watching the film. They were then asked, "Given this feeling, please list all the things you would like to do *right now.*" Those who'd seen the positive emotion films, "Penguins" and "Nature," not only had a greater number of things they wanted to do, but *what* they wanted to do was more upbeat. They wanted to be active, go outdoors, and in the case of those who saw "Penguins," to be playful and social.

The negative film viewers showed a narrow mind-set, reporting fewer urges to be active. In the case of both "Witness" and "Cliffhanger," participants reported fewer urges to eat or drink, to do schoolwork or regular work, or to reminisce with others. The "Witness" viewers showed more urges to be antisocial, and the "Cliffhanger" viewers showed a tendency to affiliate with others, perhaps a sign that participants recognized that there is safety in numbers.

The participants were also given tests designed to measure their ability to think broadly. It was a comparison of graphic figures. There is no right or wrong answer, but one choice indicates a more *big-picture* view of the world while the other is more narrow and detailed. The people who saw the positive film clips (joyful penguins and tranquil nature scenes) scored higher on broad thinking compared with those who saw the negative and neutral films.[10]

THANK YOU POWER
*Rent a funny video, or play
with the puppies at the pet shop.*

Remember, the key finding of both of these experiments was that the positive emotions promoted more expansive thinking. Because they've already focused on the good things that have happened before in their lives, grateful people naturally have a large and very full basket of positive memories to draw upon. In Anne Hjelle's case, that was a huge component in her ability to recover from her devastating experience while mountain biking.

THE POWER TO HEAL

Philip Watkins has never met Ms. Hjelle, but he might say she is a textbook example of what he's discovered in his own research on Thank You Power. Watkins, a professor of psychology at Eastern Washington State University, has researched the role gratitude plays in the ability to recall positive events from one's life.

> *A pleasure is full*
> *grown only when*
> *it is remembered.*
> —C. S. LEWIS

He has found that grateful people tend to recall *more* positive events and to recall them more easily.

Watkins was interested in seeing just how much past traumatic events haunted people. He calls it an *open memory*.

First, everyone was given a test to assess basic gratitude levels. Then the group was asked to identify their negative open memory. One group was asked to recall for twenty minutes as many positive events in their lives as possible. If at any moment an open memory popped into their minds, they were asked to tick off a box. A control group was asked to write about what they were going to do the next day, and if they ran out of things to talk about, just write about what their shoes looked like. The third group was asked to think about the open memory, having been prepped with instructions suggesting, "We know this is a difficult memory and are sure it arouses many negative emotions. Some people can think of positive consequences from a negative event, so we'd like you to write about things you can now be grateful for."

Two findings were quite clear. The grateful people were able to recall more positive events in their lives. They were also able to find more benefits from their past trauma. There was even some evidence to suggest that grateful people actually had more positive events in their lives. Watkins says, "It's not just that good events in your life make you more happy and make you more grateful. It's also that there is good suggestive data that being a grateful person is going to bring more positive things into your life. It's self-fulfilling. People like being around happy or grateful people."[11]

That would be Anne Hjelle. Spend ten minutes with her and you know she is a naturally upbeat person. She laughs as she tells the story of how she spontaneously joined the marines when she was nineteen. "I figured if I'm gonna do it, I want to go with what I think is the hardest branch of the service, you know, to really have a sense of accomplishment."

Lying on the trail, bleeding, Anne's thoughts were on her husband, James. They were supposed to celebrate their third wedding anniversary in five days. They didn't have a lifetime of memories yet. Anne says, "My first thought was *my face is ripped off. I want to die.* But my next thought was of my husband. I just couldn't imagine my life without him, and I knew for him to lose me would be devastating, so that thought changed very quickly. It was suddenly, *I have to make it through this.*"

When James got word of the accident, he rushed to the hospital, not knowing if Anne was dead or alive. When he saw her lying on the hospital gurney, he fainted—twice! The second time James went down, they put *him* on a stretcher, beside Anne. As they lay there, holding hands, Anne wasn't sure if he had fainted at relief that she was alive or at horror at what she looked like.

What Anne did know was that she already had a cadre of people praying for her. Active in her California church, she knew that members of her prayer group were praying. The good times she'd had biking flashed through her thoughts. Her bicycling buddies would be there for her. In fact, Anne told me she later learned that at what was probably the exact moment the lion pounced on her, a friend was inexplicably overcome with grief. Riding on a different trail in the park, her weeping friend was compelled to pull over and lose herself in prayer. Anne related that the friend later went back and calculated how long she'd been riding and deduced that she was led to prayer just as Anne was in the jaws of the lion.

Anne's Christian faith, the quiet confidence it gives her, and the blessings she could count from her past all contributed, she believes, to her incredible recovery. Within weeks of her attack, she and James started a Web site not only chronicling her recovery but also raising money for a foundation in memory of Mark Reynolds. It continues his tradition of providing bicycles to children who otherwise wouldn't have one. Within months Anne was on television, talking about her survival story. Soon she was speaking in front of groups.[12]

Anne's Thank You Power has helped her move emotionally past the trauma on the bike trail. Dr. Watkins says he's not surprised. "By focusing on the things we are grateful for, even during a bad event we don't understand, it helps us understand the event better. In a nutshell, gratitude helps us take care of the emotional business of negative things in our lives."[13]

Anne tells me she is proof of that. "I do believe that a thankful person attracts good in their lives," she says. "I have seen how my mind-set has changed my own reality. The scars are still there, but I have nothing to be sad or angry about. I'm alive and well."[14]

I asked Watkins if, potentially, Thank You Power could be one of the tools used to help trauma survivors cope. He said he thought so. He explained that when his study looked at the impact of a difficult past experience, for people familiar with Thank You Power, "the memory was less intrusive. It had more positive emotional impact on the grateful folks. It didn't pop up to haunt them."[15]

Thank You Power helped close the book on some pretty rough moments in people's lives. Impressive, isn't it?

THANK YOU POWER
*Spend five minutes listing as many
positive life events as possible.*

five

Give Thanks for the Bad—
Praise Your Problems

There is no disaster that
can't become a blessing . . .
—RICHARD BACH

EMMA ROTHBRUST DOES NOT LOOK AT THE DISASTER that hit her life as a blessing, but she does know she has been blessed. Her story horrified people in her hometown near Kansas City and haunted television viewers who saw the news reports about it.

It was a fall Friday night during Emma's junior year in high school. She and her friend Ashley Wanger were on their way home. Ashley was driving. Suddenly, from out of nowhere, a police car in hot pursuit came barreling down the street. Traveling eighty to ninety miles an hour, the cops blew through a red light.

The squad car's dash-cam video later showed that the stoplight had been red for at least fifteen seconds before the officers reached the intersection. Ashley had the right-of-way. But that didn't matter. The final video images are of Emma's face, eyes wide open, her hands instinctively rising to her face in horror.

Mercifully, Emma doesn't remember any of this. She remembers her mother dropping her off at Ashley's house and then waking up in intensive care just before being wheeled into surgery. Friends who saw what happened in between would say it's a good thing she doesn't remember. They were sure both girls would be brought out of the wreckage in body bags. Emma nearly was.

Miraculously, Ashley suffered only cuts and bruises, but Emma's injuries were another story. The sixteen-year-old suffered a shattered pelvis; fractures to the tibia, fibula, and ankles; a punctured uterus and fallopian tubes, and damage to her ovaries, her bladder, and a kidney. She also had a bruised liver and heart, a perforated diaphragm, and a collapsed right lung. Emma was in the hospital for more than a month. Once she was able to return to school, she attended classes in a wheelchair. For a while doctors weren't sure if Emma would ever walk again. They're still not certain if she'll be able to have children.

The accident rearranged Emma and her family's world as much as it rearranged her body. A former junior-high cheerleader who ran three miles a day, Emma now spends every single day dealing with pain. Yet, incredibly, for someone with the hip injuries she sustained, she can walk. You don't have to talk with Emma for very long to know she is one very determined young woman.

"No one ever told me I wouldn't be able to walk, but that's what everyone seemed so upset about. If you have a crushed pelvis," she explained, "you just never hear of anyone recovering all the way from that. So, I just decided that I was going to walk."

Emma walks with a limp. She can't run or jog. She can't even stand for very long. Now a college freshman, she is thrilled just to be able to sit through all of her classes. In the beginning, that simply wasn't possible. Her right side is atrophied from the impact of the crash, which, coupled with an oddly mending pelvis, means that she's a bit lopsided on her bottom. But Emma's figured out a practical way to deal with that: "I just put my cell phone in my right butt pocket and even myself out. Nobody notices!"

Her matter-of-fact retelling of her accident and the long road back to health might lead one to believe that she's just naturally optimistic. Don't be fooled.

"Funny thing about 'positive' people like that," she says. "They are not really like that. When I was stuck in bed, I knew I would have pain the next day. I was always excited to have people come to visit me. But then they would leave, and I would have a little bit of resentment. You know, like, you can sit down and then stand up and walk away. And I can't." Then, as if forcibly pushing those negative thoughts out of the room, Emma continues matter-of-factly, "But I attribute that to the numerous painkillers I was on. They kind of shift your mood around."

> *Don't pray when it rains
> if you don't pray
> when the sun shines.*
> —LEROY "SATCHEL" PAIGE

It's clear that Emma's determined mind-set has been a key asset in her recovery. She gives a lot of credit to the visitors who came to see her, many of whom she didn't even know.

"Lying in bed all day and being in pain, there's nothing really you can do. They came in just to visit me. That kind of stuff really kept me going. Even random people. I had no idea who they were. But they came. In normal life, that wouldn't be a big deal—people coming to visit. But, oh no! It was *really* a big deal."

Emma is grateful for one constant during those dark first days: her mom. Mrs. Rothbrust stayed with her daughter round the clock, nursing her, consoling her, counseling her. Emma's dad had to work, but he brought breakfast every morning and checked in on Emma each day. Emma has tried to let those who came to see her know what their gift of time meant to her.

"Some of those people I have gone back to and said, 'Wow, thank you so much for visiting me. I was so bored that day!' And I have tried to add all those people who prayed for me to *my* prayers. It's only fair," she explains. "They put all that time and energy and intense faith into me. They deserve to get it back."

Gratitude returned by gratitude. Prayer repaid by more prayers.

Asked if there is any silver lining to her horrible tragedy, Emma is quick to answer, "I'm alive. I really should be dead, and I am not, and there is something I have to do, I guess."

What that is, the girl who tried to live right, do no wrong, get good grades, and make her parents proud, can't say. A good person before, Emma says she thinks she is now better at helping others. "I think when you suffer a whole lot, you are more in tune with other people and their feelings. I think that this is part of God's purpose, but I am not sure. I am only eighteen."

Only eighteen, but wise way beyond that.

"Preaccident, I was a nice person, for sure." Emma tries to articulate a certain knowing that she possesses. "Now I can just see people and tell they are upset or in pain. I know that a smile can make you feel better about anything—even if it is for just that minute. You have that one minute: I feel better. Somebody smiled at me!"

As inconsequential as a smile may seem, Emma says the significance can be huge. She also affirms that reaching out to others when you are hurting yourself can have awesome results. "When you are in a bad mood and you see someone else in a bad mood, you try to cheer them up, and it ends up cheering you up too," she explains. "You didn't even think about that happening. But you shouldn't help others because you think things will get better for you in the end. Selfish acts don't come back to repay you. Only selfless acts do."

Emma Rothbrust is strikingly free of emotional baggage from her accident. She credits her faith for that. And she has no rancor toward the police officers responsible for her injuries.

"I am not bitter toward them," she says. "They didn't plan on hurting anybody. They were just doing their jobs, though the way they did their job could be considered questionable."[1] So questionable that the local district attorney pressed criminal charges against the two officers, the first time officers on duty had ever been charged. One pled no contest; the other worked out a plea agreement. Neither will ever be a cop again. Kansas City-area police departments have restricted their chase policies as a result of the accident. Emma's family reached an out-of-court settlement with the town where the offending cops worked.

Meanwhile, Emma, a linguistics major, says she has a message for anyone who is suffering: "Don't focus on yourself. Focus on tomorrow, and know that no matter what, it will be OK. Keep living in the moment, and be grateful for the little things. For the people being there, for the sandwich in front of you. The little things . . . the little things are best. Focus on the little things, and the days will pass until you feel better."

THANK YOU POWER
Envision the life you'd like.

Emma has been incredibly resilient in her recovery. Had she taken a resiliency-measurement test before the accident, I suspect she would have scored high. Though she doesn't call it that, Emma has been practicing Thank You Power since she was a little girl. For years she has regularly sent her mom and dad gratitude letters that she calls *love notes*. These days they take the form of e-mails expressing how much she loves them and appreciates all they've done for her—both pre- and postaccident.[2]

Emma has also been giving thanks to God for everything that has happened. She writes in an e-mail:

I can't change what happened to me and I don't want to change it—so I thank God every day for allowing me to have had such a life-changing experience. Obviously I am meant for something specific and I am grateful that God has kept me around so that I can accomplish whatever it is that He wants me to do. After all, HE was the driving force for my recovery and the driving force for my entire family's faith. He gave me strength (and not just physical strength).[3]

Emma's faith and her practice of Thank You Power were firmly in place before her automobile accident. Her faith has been a tremendous asset in her recovery. The *thank you*s that were once a silly-sweet ritual when she was a girl have been a life preserver as this young woman has dealt with challenges that would unravel the rest of us.

Many people are undone by crisis. Grateful people aren't. For example, not only do grateful folks recover faster from cardiovascular stress in experiments like the speech test described in chapter 4, but they also are stronger outside the lab as well.

THE POWER OF RESILIENCE

After the terror attacks of September 11, people who had previously been identified as resilient were half as likely to be depressed as the rest of the population. Seventy-two percent of Americans were depressed post-9/11. Researchers went back to people who'd scored high on resiliency at the beginning of the year. Not only were they handling the 9/11-associated sadness better, but many of those resilient people actually had more positive emotions during those traumatic weeks following the attack. Even more exciting, the researchers found, "low-resilient individuals can benefit from . . . positive emotions during the coping process."[4] In other words, even if Thank You Power isn't a regular part of one's life, the person who looks for and counts the blessings he or she can find, will weather a crisis better.

The ability to find positive meaning even during those frightening days following the attack is what seemed to make the difference. Rather than focus on the horror of the lives lost and the shock that America was under siege, resilient people focused on the nation's renewed patriotism, the outpouring of charity, and the concern for one another that was widely expressed at the time.

It's what got Ellen Niven through those dark days. She became a young widow on September 11, when her handsome husband, John, was among those killed. He was inside his office at the World Trade Center when the planes slammed into the towers. Ellen's son was just a toddler, whose memories of his dad will forever be only those prompted by old videos and photos.

It wasn't easy, but Ellen got through those awful days. It helped to know that her friends were sneaking through the security lines near the demolished buildings, trying to get photos of John into the hands of the search-and-rescue people. Ellen looked at her little boy and was grateful that she had a child. Her husband, she knew,

> *He is a man of sense who does not grieve for what he has not, but rejoices in what he has.*
> —EPICTETUS

would live on through him. She even watched friends whose marriages had ended in divorce and found herself grateful: alone as she was, at least she wasn't dealing with the heartbreak of rejection.

Five years after the attack, Ellen has moved forward with her life. She has remarried and had two more children. Where once she was overwhelmed with questions of how she'd manage by herself, she now sees everyday hassles as blessings—how to arrange the living room furniture and how late she and her new husband can visit a cocktail party before rushing home to relieve the babysitter. *How wonderful it is*, she thinks, *to have these kinds of problems.*[5]

Experts call this *adaptive coping*, and people who've been practicing Thank You Power prior to an adversity are better at it. The connections and personal bonds that have been emphasized during their regular gratitude checks offer strength both during and after a crisis. For grateful people, the posttraumatic stress of terrifying events is also lessened.[6] Thank You Power isn't only psychological. People in positive mind-sets have stronger immune systems, are less likely to get sick during stressful times, and can, in fact, live as much as ten years longer, simply because they tend to describe life's events in a more positive way.[7] For grateful people like Emma Rothbrust and Ellen Niven, the unpleasant will tend to fade faster, according to Philip Watkins's research.

THANK YOU POWER
Find a blessing in something bad.

Watkins's research also underscored something critical. The blessings people counted in his studies were usually not very exciting. In fact, some of them were downright boring. Three square meals a day, clean air to breathe, and a bed to sleep in are things most of us enjoy but few ever acknowledge.[8] Watkins says Thank You Power allows one to "savor the good in life, even if the good isn't very flashy."

Watkins also says that while he and others in the field have no evidence yet, he suspects that gratitude enhances people's ability to bond. He says its opposite, ingratitude, is a repellent. "People really do not like ungrateful people," he states, referring to his research. "When you look at likability ratings, gratitude is somewhere in the top 10 percent. Ingratitude is in the bottom 3 percent of disliked traits. People really dislike people who are ungrateful and, by definition, pretty much aren't going to spend much time with them."[9]

THANK YOU POWER
Cut the whine.

"Paralyzed bodies don't come with driver's manuals."

Pretty much all of his life, Chuck Adams has been writing his life's instruction manual. As for "second chances," that's what he's been working for since birth, because his first chance shouldn't count. Chuck came into this world with a severed spine, thanks to a delivery-room mishap. The doctors told Chuck's mother that he'd probably not make it into his twenties. Mrs. Adams simply replied, "You don't know me."

A fighting spirit is probably the greatest gift Chuck's parents have given him. He says it's what's gotten him this far in life. Now fifty-one, Chuck has lived his life on wheels—two big, and two small. He says his wheelchair is the equivalent of someone else's eyeglasses. He is paralyzed from the waist down.

As a little boy, Chuck never missed an episode of *Ironside*, the 1960s and '70s television show starring Raymond Burr as the wheelchair-bound detective who never let his disability keep him from catching the bad guy. Chuck's mom used to remind him that Franklin D. Roosevelt ran the war from a wheelchair.

Chuck's parents fought to get him into public school. He says he was the first wheelchair-bound student ever to go through the Mattituck, Long Island, New York school district. During those years, he remembers playing the role of the king in a school play. "My wheelchair made a splendid throne," he recalls.

Chuck Adams has other memories of childhood that have spurred him ahead in life. "The long, thin tables; the doctors; the nurses; would-be doctors, herded around me, examining my body like some case history in a textbook," he told me. "I was just another body to them." Later, Chuck was taken to the Rusk Institute, a rehabilitation center—just for a visit—and was shattered by what he saw. "I couldn't believe how they were all so resigned to failure. The patients had no drive. No ambition. They were so willing to settle for less." It only steeled Chuck's resolve to reach for something more.

> *A grateful person trusts enough to give life another chance, to stay open for surprises.*
> —BROTHER DAVID STEINDAL-RAST

Something More. Those words have special resonance for Chuck. It's the title of a book and screenplay he's written that he hopes to one day share with a wide audience. It is his story with a romantic twist. I won't spoil it by outlining it here. But what I will reveal is a story of a man who refuses to stay down, though the Fates—and sometimes other people—seem to conspire against him. The conspirators never win because Chuck has a special perspective.

Chuck says that early on his parents taught him to count his blessings, that there was always someone worse off. Sitting in all those clinics was proof enough of that. For forty years the spirit of Thank You Power has helped Chuck Adams acknowledge all that's good in his life and propel him forward, toward achievements that the delivery-room doctor would have never imagined. For example, he was the captain of his college wheelchair basketball team. His work life has been varied and fulfilling, including managing huge retail stores and serving as a marketing executive at a financial institution. He has also worked as a journalist for his local paper and hosted a cable sports show. Today, Chuck is the proud (and sometimes harried!) father of two daughters. In short, Chuck has spent the last forty years living. He does so with a fervor that may be driven by his determination to never be like those forlorn souls he saw years ago as a kid.

"I have an unquenchable thirst, a passion for life. I've learned you have to make things happen. So often, people settle. Too often, we're afraid to reach for that brass ring, to chase our dreams," Chuck tells me. "But I've decided my self-worth is not dependent on whether I see the world standing or sitting. When I talk to schoolkids about disabilities, I tell them success is more often derived, not from your arms and legs, but from your heart and head."[10]

I met Chuck about seven or eight years ago when he was in the retail business. Obviously, he was the guy in the wheelchair, but what stood out about Chuck was his intensity. At the time he was managing a superstore in Long Island, and he ran a tight ship. He was also very much looking ahead to the next challenge, whatever it might be.

Incredible as it sounds, Chuck says he has never prayed that someday he would walk. Instead, he says, "I am grateful for what I have. I have the ability to figure things out. I have a bottomless reservoir of resiliency, of strength. I have learned to let go of the things I have no control over."

I think Muhammad Ali would call Chuck Adams a winner. Chuck says with pride, "The seeds we plant do resonate with our children as they mature." His daughters are now out of high school.

> *Only a man who knows what it is like to be defeated can reach down to the bottom of his soul and come up with the power it takes to win.*
> —MUHAMMAD ALI

One daughter donated a foot of her hair to an organization that makes wigs for kids with cancer. His other daughter volunteers to read to children at the local library. Both girls have spent weekends making crafts that they later donated to an orphanage or nursing home. Having a dad in a wheelchair, Adams says, has given his girls a different perspective on life.

Chuck's goal now is to help others have a fresh perspective on people with disabilities, perhaps with that screenplay he's writing. Over time, Chuck Adams has decided that different is neither better nor worse; it's just, well, different. If grateful people do trust life enough to give it a second chance, Chuck has an endless supply of both gratitude and trust. He knows how easy it would have been to give in to the doubters who early on predicted a short life of hardship. He is justifiably proud of how wrong he proved them. And each time either he or his wheelchair hits one of those small bumps in life's road, Chuck is renewed by his long list of accomplishments. He is reenergized in knowing that for him, there is something more.[11]

THANK YOU POWER
*Focus on a bad situation and
how you turned it around.*

six

Stop Staring in the Mirror—
Look Out the Window Instead

*Happiness is a by-product of
an effort to make someone else happy.*
—GRETTA PALMER

WANT TO FEEL REALLY GOOD ABOUT YOURSELF? DO something for someone else.

The Schuster Performing Arts Center in Dayton, Ohio, is an impressive facility. Plenty of cities four times the size of Dayton don't have concert halls even half as nice. Schuster is a sparkling edifice with vaulted ceilings, private luncheon rooms, musician practice halls, and an acoustically precise performance hall that guarantees that there is not a bad seat in the house. But the real jewel at the performing arts center is backstage—her name is Kim.

I met Kim when I was invited by the Dayton Junior League to

speak for two days during their Town Hall Lecture Series. It's always a bit scary to speak in front of these groups. I get invited to lecture often, but, though I have been delivering speeches for years (and talk to about five million people daily on television), I *always* have a bit of performance anxiety.

Will my message hit home? Can I leave folks with information that will be useful to them *after* they leave? Will they hate themselves for having spent their morning at the Deborah Norville lecture? My hope every single time is that the guests will go home happy, feeling that they learned something and didn't waste their very precious time.

> *A person starts to live when he lives outside himself.*
> —ALBERT SCHWEITZER

As I recall, the Dayton speeches went great. Attendees laughed at the right times, gasped when I thought they'd be stunned, and even gave me a standing ovation when I finished. They had smiles on their faces, so I think they stood and clapped because they liked what I had to say (but you never know—maybe they just had fanny fatigue!).

That's what I recall. What I remember with crystal clarity is Kim Keough, the stage manager. She was the wizard who ruled behind the curtain. She was there to make sure I didn't miss my cue to walk onstage. You could tell she was a woman who knew her stuff, a true professional. You know how sometimes you meet someone and you realize that you just connect? Kim was that kind of person. With her, I felt an instant rapport. Sometimes with people like that, their nonverbal messages speak much louder than anything they say.

To me, Kim was a girl who'd become *one of the guys*. She was a tall, striking woman with thick, blonde hair and sharp, blue eyes that refused to be muted by her wire-framed glasses. When I say she had become one of the guys, I know you know what I mean. She'd been working behind the scenes at the theater, keeping order backstage, and honchoing the installation of theatrical sets and orchestra seats for so long that she'd gradually given up taking care of the beautiful woman hiding beneath the T-shirt and jeans.

The uniform had been adopted of necessity. No sensible woman would risk a gorgeous blouse being ripped as huge scenery flats were hauled across the stage. But I also sensed that the T-shirt and tennis shoes had become a refuge for Kim, and for some reason that I still can't put my finger on, I felt as if that refuge had become a prison. She was becoming such a guy that she was losing the girl within.

Grateful Deb—who was at risk of becoming buttinski Deb—decided to intervene. My chance came, thanks to the shoes.

Those Junior League ladies were dressed to a tee: great makeup and hair, pretty spring suits, and some fancy-looking footwear. Those pumps were something! The officers who'd be making remarks onstage were lined up, and you couldn't help but notice the shoes: high, shiny, and really sexy. The ladies laughed about how badly their feet hurt, but we all agreed: at times you have to suffer for beauty. Each of us might be enduring pain, but we felt like a million bucks wearing such cool shoes.

I thought Kim—with her height and fabulous long legs hidden beneath those Levis—would look amazing with a pair of superhot pumps. With some time to kill while the Junior League ladies were doing their thing onstage, I nudged her. "You are letting all these guys around here ride roughshod on you. Just 'cause they're guys doesn't mean *you* have to be. Embrace your femininity," I urged. "You are a beautiful woman, but you are hiding it!"

I nodded toward her sneakers. "Now, those shoes, for instance," and I was off. "I know there are times when you have to wear tennis shoes when you're moving sets in and out. But today's a no-brainer day. All you've got to do is kick me out on the stage at the right time."

I took my pump off and put it beside her pant leg. "See how cool these shoes look with your jeans? And that white T-shirt is perfect. Just throw a blazer over it and you are Miss Super Chic." And before Kim could make the "shoes are expensive" argument, I headed her off at the pass.

"Look, you don't have to spend a bundle on shoes. You can hit Payless and get some great shoes on your way home tonight. Or check out some catalogs. I got an amazing pair of black suede pumps for thirty dollars! Your husband will never notice you've spent the money." I paused for effect. "What he *will* notice is the awesome woman who comes sashaying in at the end of the day."

Buttinski Deb was now becoming Pastor Deborah. "Kim, it's obvious from the way you interact with the guys here that everyone really likes you. But you are blending into the scenery, and I can tell you are just too special to do that. You are *not* one of the boys! You are a *woman*, and these dudes need to be reminded of that." I lowered my voice a bit. "And maybe you need to remind *yourself* too."

I didn't tell Kim this, but I'll tell you. When I am feeling really down, there are three things that I can do that make me feel instantly better. One is eating potato chips or cookie dough. (I sometimes mention cookie-dough therapy in my speeches, and it's amazing how many people know *exactly* what I'm talking about. Raw slice-and-bake can provide instant relief, but you hate yourself later for eating it.)

Another is hitting the warehouse shopping club. There is something about buying forty-eight rolls of toilet paper in one package that gives me enormous pleasure. Never mind that a single person living alone would conservatively take more than three years to use that much. (That is roughly fifty thousand sheets if you are doing the math. The trouble with Price Club therapy is when you live in a New York apartment, there really isn't any place to put your purchases.)

Number three is what I had in mind as I talked with Kim: doing something for herself. For me, that means makeup. When I am really down in the dumps, sometimes just washing my face and starting over makeup-wise is a great emotional lift. Maybe I feel prettier; maybe it's that the focus required to apply the cosmetics is calming—either way, it works for me. And I do think all of us, men and women, have a higher sense of self-confidence if we believe we present well to the outside world.

I looked at Kim. She really *was* pretty—but it was easy to overlook her beauty. And I feared that people were also overlooking Kim.

"Promise me—before the week is out—that you'll try the pumps. You can keep the sneakers here and put 'em on when you need 'em, but give the pumps a go."

"We'll see . . ." she said, noncommittally. But she was smiling! Then Kim was mercifully saved by the cue to send me out to the stage, ending my intervention.

The next day, I was back at the convention center. The Junior League ladies were again looking fabulous. They were still wearing their fine footwear. Only this time, there was one more pair of hot-looking shoes backstage: Kim's. On her way home from work the night before, Kim had stopped at Nordstrom's and found a supersexy pair of shoes on sale. I forget what she paid, but whatever the price, it wasn't just a shoe purchase. It was an investment—in herself.

THANK YOU POWER
Do something for someone else—
no thanks expected or accepted!

I can't tell you how good I felt when I saw Kim in her brand-spanking-new pumps. But I felt even better when I got my most recent e-mail from Sal Morales.

I have never met Sal, but I know him better than some of the people I see every day. Sal and I met over the Internet. (No, not *that* way!) He e-mailed me out of the blue, having stumbled across my Web site one night while surfing the Net.

Sal was unemployed and hugely depressed. He had lost his job in Los Angeles, couldn't find another, and had depleted his savings to the point that he had to move back home to Miami and live with his parents. For years, he had worked in television, moving from nice-sized markets like Atlanta to even bigger markets like San Francisco and finally to Los Angeles. One of his happiest days was just after September 11, when he was made a part of the news team on the Telemundo morning news show, *Buenos Días Los Angeles.* Sal was the Al Roker of the program, the meteorologist who also did light features. It was the job Sal had always dreamed of and worked for years to deserve. It also had some pretty cool perks: since Telemundo was owned by NBC, Sal had his own parking spot on the NBC lot—right where Jay Leno and Deidre Hall parked *their* cars.

Television being what it is, however, the gig didn't last. Management had other ideas and changed the format. Sal was told he had no job.

"I was told my career was over at Telemundo, to disappear and go away—after almost ten years!" To say that Sal's world was upended hardly does justice to what he went through. It is still painful for him to talk about. "I honest to God didn't feel any hope," he related to me. "When I had to leave my job, I went through a deep depression and had to be taken to the emergency room, it was so bad. For two days, I was catatonic. I was stunned. You would talk to me, and I would not know who you were."[1]

It was hard to hear a man talk about being so vulnerable. I had a vision of this man, vacantly staring into space in a spare white room somewhere between *One Flew over the Cuckoo's Nest* and *Grey's Anatomy*. I was thinking, *You have to be in pretty bad shape to be hospitalized for depression!* It must have been just awful.

Lucky for Sal, he is from a close-knit family. Thick or thin, they are there for one another. Sal hadn't lived close to home in years, but his sister and mother flew to California and told him it was time to change that. "You're coming home," his sister said. She called the movers and took care of everything.

"She said, 'You are my brother. I will help you,'" Sal recalled. "She said, 'You think that Telemundo was your whole life, that you achieved stardom, and now it was taken away from you.'" Sal continued, "She also said something very true: She said I was not fighting with anybody. I was fighting with myself."

With his sister's help, Sal packed his stuff; his cat, Clovis; and a whole bunch of mixed-up thoughts and moved back home to mom and dad. For a man approaching his fortieth birthday, it was a hideously embarrassing state of affairs. And he was still fixated on television. Night after night, he would spend hours on the computer, reading about the media business and googling TV personalities.

One night he stumbled across a Wikipedia entry about my own long-ago troubles in television and eventually clicked through to my Web site.[2] While on my home page, he saw this little blurb:

It is rainy today in New York . . . the kind of misty rain that hangs rather than falls. Driving to work after an appointment, we had to wait to make our turn because of a man crossing the sidewalk. He was a quadriplegic, maneuvering his wheelchair with each exhale of breath. Heedless of the mist—and unable to do anything about it anyway, he maneuvered over the curb.

I was simultaneously struck by both his grace in moving through his challenging life . . . and filled with gratitude that I haven't been given that cross to bear. I said a quick thank you to the man upstairs.

I find myself expressing gratitude like that many times each day—and I believe my life is richer for it.

What role does gratitude play in your life? I'd love to hear from you!

—Deborah[3]

That little moment in time that I captured on my Web site prompted Sal to write. I remember two things about his initial e-mail: how totally despondent he sounded, and the weight of the fact that he had reached out to *me*. How could I possibly help this man who was clearly reaching to a total stranger for a lifeline?

Sal had written very briefly that despite his experience as a Los Angeles TV weatherman, he was having no luck getting any kind of TV job in Miami. He also wrote that he was about to take a job teaching Spanish at Berlitz just so he'd have something to do. Later he told me that he was also applying for a job at Starbucks because he'd heard they offered health insurance. Sal spoke of his disappointment at approaching forty, out of work, and with no place of his own. Though I had no way of knowing the mental health issues he'd dealt with earlier, I could tell I was hearing from a man on the edge. Sal was not one of the crazies—and trust me, I hear from plenty of them—but a man who truly did not know which way to turn.[4]

It took me right back to a dark time in my own television career. I knew what Sal was putting himself through, agonizing over the dream job that turned to dust. But unlike Sal, I knew the agony would end. He'd move on with his life and eventually even find that what he was doing post-TV trauma was pretty darn terrific. But I knew better than to tell Sal that. Instead, I just told him what to do.

I e-mailed back and reminded him that he was in the number one Hispanic media market in the nation. That if the TV people in Miami didn't see his talent, chances were the radio people would. I told him radio people are often a little bit envious of the guys on the television side, sometimes even a bit in awe. I said, "You play that TV card for all it's worth and contact every Spanish-speaking radio station in town and get in there for an interview."

Before Sal could ask what he was interviewing for, I gave him his cover story. After years away from home, he decided to come back to Miami for family reasons. Now, this *is* true though the whole truth is his family needed him back home so they could take care of Sal. No need for the station people to know that, right? I told Sal he should just say now that things were settled on the home front (again, true: he was doing *much* better), he was ready to get back to work.

Well, I believe Sal spoke to every Hispanic station in town. And wouldn't you know, not one had any openings. It wasn't that he was too qualified or too high priced (I am sure Sal was very negotiable salary-wise); there simply weren't any on-air jobs at any of the stations.

But while he was out pounding the pavement, Sal heard about a television station that *wasn't* on the air—yet. WSBS-TV22 was the first TV station owned by Spanish Broadcasting Systems, which holds a chain of radio stations around the country. Mega-TV didn't have a news department or a weathercast, and it didn't have a lot of money for salaries either. What it did have was an executive who had been Sal's boss years ago when he was an intern. She told Sal, "You are a news guy. We aren't going to have news. What I need is help organizing PR."

After all those weeks of selling himself to those radio stations, Sal knew he could sell a TV station to the viewers.

I got an excited e-mail from Sal, announcing his new job. All the while, I was wondering how on earth he was going to market the station. I zapped back a reply: "Go to all those radio stations you just met. The radio guys are always looking for ways to promote their product, and your new station represents a terrific opportunity for them." Sal agreed that all that pounding of pavement he'd done in looking for a job was now a gigantic asset for Mega-TV. He brainstormed a clever PR pitch with me that involved Chinese takeout boxes and fortune cookies—*not* what you'd expect from a Hispanic station and *definitely* something that would stand out in the swamp of publicity materials the stations received.

Today Sal has more than a job in television. He told me, "I have my dignity back. I have developed into something I never thought I would be able to. I can work. I am not just a bumbling zero. I can do press releases. I can convince people to do things with my station."

Now Sal has interns who report to him, and he's beginning to mentor other young Hispanics who aspire to break into the business. He says it's because he loves his job. "This is the first time in my life that I don't have a stomachache when I walk into the office." Sal is now talking so fast I can hardly keep up. "I don't walk into this building; I bounce."[5]

> *Those who bring sunshine to the lives of others cannot keep it from themselves.*
> —James M. Barrie

If Sal was bouncing on just a normal day at the office, he was catapulting as Hurricane Ernesto was blowing into Miami. Since Mega-TV didn't have a news department, it did not have the staff or facilities to keep its viewers informed of important information they needed to know as the storm approached. Sal says he connected with the folks at the local CBS station and worked a cooperative deal in which he'd provide the forecasts in Spanish to Mega-TV viewers, using information from Channel 4. Each station would cross promote to turn to the other for more information.

After the storm passed through, I got another enthusiastic e-mail from Sal. "I was back on television!" he exclaimed. "It was just to get us through the hurricane, but I was *back*!" Sal ended his e-mail by saying that he was going to start working out and losing the weight he'd put on during unemployment.[6] As I closed Sal's e-mail, I said to myself, *I see pancake makeup in that man's future!*

What I didn't see was the Emmy nomination. Here's the e-mail Sal just sent me:

Dear Deborah:

Guess what???? I have been nominated for an Emmy in South Florida as best weather reporter! We did a special here at Mega-TV regarding preparations for Miami during this hurricane season. We did it with no resources, not even a Chroma. I did the standups on Biscayne Bay, overlooking the downtown skyline. We provided info in very basic terms so newcomers can see what the severity of a hurricane can be.

The nominations were announced last week, and among them was my name. I have been nominated twice—back in Los Angeles for consumer reporting—and didn't get the award. Even if I don't win, I am sooo happy! God works in very, very mysterious ways indeed. Good nite.

Adios,

Sal[7]

Yes, God *does* work in mysterious ways.

A few months after Sal started his new job, I saw the TV station's announcement in the trades about his position, and I sent it to him. When we spoke on the phone, I told him that announcement had made me feel more proud than any of the press releases I'd ever seen about myself. Here's what he said in reply:

"I cannot believe that. I am honored. You know, I gotta tell you, I reached out and I actually found an angel. I decided to write [to] you, and the next thing, I was reading an e-mail from Deborah Norville. My sister said, 'You're joking.' And ever since then, I have actually believed in myself and in God again.

"That passage about that man in a wheelchair told me to look for other avenues. That I could actually look for a little window of hope. And hope, or *esperanza*, as we say in Spanish, is something to hold on to."[8]

> *The truth is that our finest moments are most likely to occur when we are feeling deeply uncomfortable, unhappy, or unfulfilled. For it is only in such moments, propelled by our discomfort, that we are likely to step out of our ruts and start searching for different ways or truer answers.*
> —SCOTT PECK

I cannot explain any of this. But I know the story is true. And I know every time I think of Sal Morales and the beautiful journey he is now on, I feel that my own road gets a bit easier too.

That Scott Peck quote just seemed to be written for Sal Morales. Sal has had higher-profile moments during his life. It is a big deal to be a weatherman in Los Angeles. But I suspect there haven't been any finer moments than the recent experiences you've just read about. From his own discomfort and despair, Sal stepped out, looking for truth. I think he's found it.

Chances are you're feeling pretty good right now. Sal's story is one of hope for all of us. Bad times can end. Words of hope can be found in the most unlikely of places. Simply being there for someone else can be powerful.

Just hearing about someone else's good deed is good for you. Sal makes it pretty clear that he's enjoying the benefits of the encouragement he got from me. You don't need a rocket-science degree to appreciate how uplifted and gratified *I feel* hearing Sal talk about his future.

But you, dear reader, are benefiting as well. University of Virginia associate professor of psychology Dr. Jonathan Haidt says the good deed helps everyone. He calls it *elevation*, the lifting of emotions for anyone who witnesses or hears about a positive act and a desire to act on those emotions. Haidt credits the founder of his university, Thomas Jefferson, for being one of the first to call attention to the phenomenon:

> *When any . . . act of charity or of gratitude,*
> *for instance, is presented to our sight*
> *or imagination, we are deeply impressed with*
> *its beauty and feel a strong desire in ourselves*
> *of doing charitable and grateful acts also.*
> —THOMAS JEFFERSON IN A 1771 LETTER

For seven years Dr. Haidt has been studying elevation, using video clips about heroes and altruism to induce good feelings. Those heartwarming, emotional moments really are literally heart warming. Test subjects report that they have a physically warm and pleasant feeling in the chest. They say they, too, want to help others or become better persons. Just asking the people to watch the clips and comment on them had a positive effect: all of the test subjects rated their moods as "better" than they were before they viewed the videos.

That chest-pointing part of the warm fuzzies intrigued Haidt and some of his students. Was the emotion they felt connected to the vagus nerve, a key nerve that calms people down and undoes the effects of the fight-or-flight hormones? The same nerve also triggers the release of the hormone oxytocin that initiates the release of breast milk in nursing mothers. So the researchers had two groups of nursing mothers, one watched Oprah Winfrey clips to elicit elevation, and the control group saw a video of a Jerry Seinfeld monologue.

Haidt says it was one of the biggest effects he's ever seen in a study. Half of the mothers in the elevation/Oprah group leaked milk or nursed their babies. Only 11 percent did in the group that watched the comedies.[9] Persuasive evidence. Haidt believes that the same nerve that helps the body deal with the ill effects of stress also plays a role when a person feels elevated by the actions of others.

Haidt believes "elevation increases the likelihood that a witness to good deeds will soon become a doer of good deeds," creating a kind of domino effect of positive acts.[10] I'd like to think that hearing of my experiences with Sal and Kim might inspire you to extend yourself on behalf of someone else. Call it Thank You Power once removed: doing something for someone else even if *you* weren't on the receiving end of a good deed.

THANK YOU POWER
What good deeds for others have you witnessed?

We all like to be appreciated. Thank You Power can be a magnet. But the degree to which people who feel appreciated will extend themselves may surprise you.

Research has shown that people who feel indebted may willingly take on pain that was intended for the person to whom they feel obligated. In one study, mild electric shocks were administered for incorrect answers. (Again, most of the test subjects in these research projects are college students at the university where the research is being conducted. There's not enough course credit in the world for me to willingly sit there and get zapped!) Not only were shocks given, but the test subjects were manipulated into feeling grateful for other individuals in the test group, so grateful that they'd take the shock *on their behalf!* Participants who were thanked for helping a confederate by accepting electric shocks for that person continued to receive shocks at a higher rate than did participants who were not thanked initially.

Talk about the impact of Thank You Power! The study was manipulated so that the person who was wired up was thanked in a way that invoked a sense of connection to the persons answering the questions. Those connections were so enhanced that the person was willing—and even offered—to take the shock for the comrade's incorrect response.[11] That's really taking one for the team! All because the person felt appreciated.

BOOMERANG POWER

Time and again, we see that *what goes around comes around*. Thank You Power, when expressed, almost always boomerangs back.

A few years ago, researchers wanted to see what the impact of *thank you* really was, using a residential treatment facility for adolescent teens. One can imagine what an emotionally draining job it must be to serve as a social worker for a teenager whose life is in such upheaval that he or she has been placed in a clinic.

The observation period began, and for five months researchers simply monitored the social workers' visits to get a baseline figure for the number of trips they made. During this time, 43 percent of the teenagers were visited by their caseworkers.

For the next five months, each time a caseworker visited a client, a representative of the residential unit sent that worker a note of thanks. During the period when thank you notes were being sent, 80 percent of the clients were visited by their case managers. At the end of that period, the letters stopped, and caseworker visitation rates dropped back to what they roughly were before: about 50 percent of the clients got a weekly visit.[12] Clearly, Thank You Power meant something to those caseworkers. People who feel appreciated are more willing to make an effort on behalf of those who make them feel valued.

In one study, waitresses who simply wrote "thank you" on the check before handing it to their customers received on average 11 percent more in tips than those who didn't.[13] Waiters who wrote a message about an upcoming dinner special on their checks also received higher tips. On average, their tips increased by 17 to 20 percent.[14] In a world where personal connections seem increasingly limited, and sometimes stressful when they do occur, Thank You Power has great resonance.

But remember what Professor Alice Isen said: grateful people aren't patsies, and they really react when they don't suspect there's an ulterior motive at work. For example, jewelry-store customers who got a call thanking them for their business spent more during return visits the follow-ing month than customers who didn't get a thank you call. But they also spent more than cus-tomers who got the thank you call *and* were told at the same time of an upcoming 20 percent-off sale. Word of the sale, which could be perceived as a pitch for more business, made the thank you ring hollow.[15]

> *If you want to lift yourself up, lift up someone else.*
> —BOOKER T. WASHINGTON

How does the boomerang effect really work? Remember Kim Keough, the house carpenter at the performing arts center in Dayton? She and I have stayed in touch. About six months after we met, I got an e-mail from her. The Junior League's Town Hall Lecture Series was gearing back up for a new season. That meant that Kim had to start getting ready. You are probably thinking that means new microphones and repainting the backdrops, right? No way! Kim told me she's been checking the newspaper ads, look-ing for something new and different in shoes or boots.

"The ladies with Town Hall expect at least one day with heels," she told me, "and so far, since you've been here, I haven't let them down."[16]

I just can't help but smile every time I think of that. At 12:26 a.m. as I am writing this, here I sit, eyes rimmed with tears and a heart filled with gratitude. Those few minutes that Kim and I had backstage clearly made a difference in her life.

She tells me that she makes a point now to remember to take a bit of extra time to put on makeup. She also says that every now and then, I pop into her head: "Just trying to remember that even though I work with men all the time, I certainly don't have to dress like them. And for that I THANK YOU."[17]

No, Kim, I thank *you*. What Kim may not appreciate is just how much she has given to me. Most of us never know whether we impact someone else's life. We simply assume we don't. Kim, thank you for the reminder that each of us, in the most ordinary of passing moments, has the power to make magic for someone else. That reminder is a gift to all of us—and for that, I am very grateful.

Nineteenth-century writer Henry David Thoreau put it this way:

To affect the quality of the day, that is the highest of arts.[18]

That's nice, but really kind of highbrow and stuffy. As a user-friendly reminder of the impact any of us can have on another, Kim and her cute shoes work just fine for me.

seven
Your Secret Garden

> *If you observe a really happy man, you will find him*
> *building a boat, writing a symphony, educating his son,*
> *growing double dahlias or looking for dinosaur eggs*
> *in the Gobi desert. He will not be searching for happiness*
> *as if it were a collar button that had rolled under*
> *the radiator striving for it as the goal itself. He will*
> *have become aware that he is happy in the course*
> *of living life twenty-four crowded hours of each day.*
>
> —W. BERAN WOLFE

BY NOW YOU SHOULD HAVE A FAIRLY LONG LIST OF ITEMS in your Thank You Power journal. If you go through them, you should see a pattern emerging. Many of your entries will underscore the importance of people in your life and your relationships with them. Others highlight experiences that continue to stand out as meaningful for some reason. The third group will be things that began with you, something you created that you can point to with pride and say, "I made that happen." Whether it's the girls' school Ann Tisch spearheaded or a blanket for a shut-in, an important source for Thank You Power is the ability to say, "I did it myself."

It's called *eudaemonia*—the happiness or fulfillment that comes from the action itself, not the result of it. In other words, the actual act of helping a person, founding a school, or knitting a sweater is a source of pleasure to the doer. Any additional bene-fit that comes—the person is grateful, the school is a success, or the sweater keeps someone warm—is just icing on the cake.

I've experienced *eudaemonia* most of my life. I just never knew it was called that. Whether it is building the headboard for my bed, knitting a cozy cap and sweater for one of my kids, or trying to cultivate a decent-looking garden, I get as much pleasure from digging, stitching, and hammering as I do from the finished prod-uct. It is, for me, a tried-and-true source of Thank You Power.

THANK YOU POWER
Use your creative side—if you have a hobby,
do *it! If you don't,* find one!

Lily Chin not only uses her creative side, but she's made a career of it. Known as the world's fastest crocheter, this New Yorker has practically set land-speed records with her fleet, flying fingers. A knitwear designer for nearly twenty-five years, Lily finds Thank You Power in every garment she creates. Talking almost as fast as she knits and crochets, she says, "I think every human has that urge to create. I think leaving a bit of yourself behind in this world is important. It's a bit of immortality." She laughs. "Some people have babies; I make sweaters.

"It's a sense of continuity in the world where everything is manufactured," Lily explains. "These are things that keep you closer to the roots with how things are made, and it gives you a better appreciation of the things we actually do have. You see a cheap garment at Wal-Mart, and you have more of an appreciation of how it's done and the work that goes into it."

Chin, the kind of kid who'd take toys apart just to see how they worked, learned to knit and crochet when she was eight. Her mother gave her a crochet needle and some yarn just to keep her rowdy daughter out of her hair. Lily was literally *hooked*. Today she is the author of a number of knitting and crochet books featuring her own patterns. She's worked with top designers, including Diane Von Furstenberg and Ralph Lauren. But she says her most meaningful work is the kind she does for the Red Scarf Project, which each year sends care baskets that include hand-made scarves to college-bound foster youth.

"There is no greater gift than . . . giving something that comes off your hand, from your brains, to your hands through your heart. When you make it and not just buy it, you give a piece of your-self." With knitting and crocheting, there is a hug in every stitch. Lily will spend part of her holiday season knitting red scarves that send hugs to kids in college.

Lily lives life with a zest most of us would envy. She travels the country, teaching others the art of knitting, and says nothing excites her more than to see them take up the craft.[1]

Finding your passion can be an important way of enhancing

your life. The Values in Strength project that Professors Chris Peterson and Martin Seligman carried out at the University of Pennsylvania concluded that of all the twenty-four signature strengths they identified, hope, zest, gratitude, curiosity, and love had the greatest ability to impact one's life. Strengths like curiosity and love of learning had noticeably less impact. The more strongly one identified with a strength, the greater life satisfaction he reported.[2]

THANK YOU POWER
Make or bake something,
and share it with someone else.

As one part of the research on signature strengths, participants were asked to identify five different strengths—you might call them your top five talents—and use one of them in some way every day for a week. The people who did this had the same elevation of mood as those in a separate group who daily tallied three things for which they were thankful.[3]

If you can find both your passion *and* a way to share it with others, you'll get twice the benefit. Dr. Martin Seligman, regarded as the founder of the field of positive psychology, says he discovered that during the first positive psychology class he ever taught. Students were asked to do one pleasurable activity and one philanthropic activity and write up their experiences. "The results were dramatic. The 'pleasurable' activities (hanging out with friends, going to a movie) paled in comparison to the effects of the kind action. When the philanthropic activity was spontaneous and called upon skill, the rest of the day went better; whereas the pleasure of the pleasurable activity faded immediately."[4]

Bob Vila knows a thing or two about building. America's master craftsman, he has been teaching the rest of us how to wield a power drill and plumb a wall for nearly thirty years. He has helped millions of Americans learn the superior feeling of satisfaction that comes from completing a project, whether it's remodeling an entire house or refinishing a piece of furniture. It has now been decades since he restored a big rolltop desk—one of his first projects—but his voice comes alive when he talks about it. He says, "It's a question of total relaxation. It allows you to unplug from everything else for a while and just focus on that particular project."

> *Beliefs are like the foundation of a building, and they are the foundation to build your own life upon.*
> —ALFRED A. MONTAPERT

The Bob Vila empire first started when he and his wife restored an old Victorian Italianate house in Newton, Massachusetts. It was the mid-1970s, and the fixer-upper craze had not yet begun. The Vila home got a little local publicity, which led to a television producer literally knocking on the door and asking to do a pilot about fixing up old houses. Bob says it was his Lana Turner moment. "It was kind of like being on a soda-fountain stool and having someone discover me," he said with a laugh. Thus was born *This Old House*.

I asked him about how the focus he gets from his creative pursuits helps in the rest of his life. Momentarily lost in thought, he responded, "Everything that has to do with bricks and mortar has a solution. I don't get too glum about physical things that might go wrong, permit inspections, or structural problems that may delay you. Obviously delays cost money. I think the things that have brought me down have been personal disappointments, relationships having to do with people in business.

"There have been situations," he continues, "where people have really shocked me with their behavior. There have been times in [my] career where [I felt] like saying, 'I want to hang this up.' Then you realize that there are all these other people who are part of your success, and they are the ones who count." Bob feels lucky to have some colleagues who've been with him for as long as twenty-five years.

But a funny thing has happened to Bob on the way to showing the rest of us how to restore things around the house: he no longer has time to do it himself. Between shooting another TV show, working on real-estate projects, and promoting his new tool line, the only time he gets to pick up a tool is to show someone else what to do with it. He says he can't remember the last time he had his own project restoring something. But that's OK. There is a creative endorphin from showing others how to do it too.

"In the end, it gives you the same level of satisfaction. Even though it's not a headboard you're leaning against at night or a desk you're working on that you refinished. It's a bit broader."[5]

Bob and I spoke the day after he had just wrapped up a shoot in St. Petersburg, Florida. The show is on new, low-income housing being built from discarded steel shipping containers. He was as animated talking about this greater-good effort as he was his new line of tools.

"There are literally hundreds of thousands of empty shipping containers that we used to bring in all the goods from China. Because we no longer manufacture anything that we can use these containers to export with, they sit around idle." Vila explained how the project uses the containers as the foundation for energy-efficient new homes. He's just a reporter of the story and has no financial interest in the effort. But the enormity of the possibilities both for the environment and for once down-on-their-luck individuals to get a new start is clearly an emotional boost. He concludes, "You are not just doing stuff for yourself. You are doing something that is for everybody, and that's what really matters."[6]

eight

Grow Where You're Planted

*I have learned from experience that the greater
part of our happiness or misery depends upon
our dispositions, and not upon our circumstances.*
—MARTHA WASHINGTON

WE ALL KNOW THAT STUFF HAPPENS. IT'S JUST NOT
supposed to happen to *us*.

Not one of us would blame the Hutto family of Tennessee for
saying that. But in the year and a half that I have known them, I
have never heard it. What I have heard is "Don't give up," "He has
never complained," "I never knew people could be so caring," and
the most frequent, "It's a miracle."

It *is* a miracle that Craig Hutto, the youngest of a family of
three athletic boys, is still alive. He came "this close" to becoming

a shark-attack statistic. It was the summer before his junior year in high school, one week before his seventeenth birthday. He and his family were in Panama City, Florida for vacation. Craig and his brother Brian were near the shore, surf fishing.

Home videos from that morning show a lanky teenager up to his knees in the water, making his first casts. His mom was comfortably relaxing in a beach chair, already enjoying a morning at the beach.

Without warning, something bumped Craig, and before he knew it, he was fighting off a shark. His brother came rushing to help him and probably saved his life. Craig's hands were severely gashed from battling the shark, and his lower leg was in shreds.

The family's screams attracted some Good Samaritans on the beach, who rendered lifesaving first aid on the spot. For his mom and dad, it seemed like an eternity before ambulances arrived at the scene to rush Craig to the emergency room. When Craig finally arrived at the hospital, doctors were forced to amputate his lower leg to save his life. Craig celebrated his birthday in the hospital.

For Craig, the horror of the accident was bad enough. But the medical people inadvertently made it worse. Craig felt as if no one would give a straight answer to the one question he had: Will I survive?

"I would ask the doctors, 'Am I gonna survive?' Because they can't lie to you; they've gotta tell the truth," Craig's voice is tightening with the tension of remembering those first days in the hospital. "They won't say yes if they don't know. And the doctors didn't know for sure if I was gonna survive. That was the thing that stressed me out the most."[1]

Stressed-out is an understatement. Craig was fixated on whether or not he would make it. He asked anyone who entered his hospital room the same question. The janitor, the nurses, the volunteer staff—anyone who came in, he asked, "Am I going to survive?" Finally, his mother recalls, one of the nurses took him by the hand and set him straight.

"She said, 'What you are going through right now, you are going to survive,'" Lou Ann Hutto related. "Then she said, 'But there is no guarantee when you walk out that door that you won't get hit by a car.'" But even when Craig was transferred to Vanderbilt Hospital, close to home, he was still obsessed. Finally his orthopedist realized that the only way Craig would understand that he *was* going to live, would be to send him home, wounds and all. Craig finally acknowledged that he was out of the woods.[2]

> *I have learned to be content in whatever circumstances I am.*
> —PHILIPPIANS 4:11 (NASB)

Out of the woods . . . but not running through them. Craig lost his right leg above the knee, and for a family in which athletics is practically one of the five daily food groups, his loss is keenly felt. When I last talked with Craig, he phoned on his cell from basketball practice. He's on the team. Not yet playing, but working to master running on his prosthesis, with hopes of getting back in the game.

I don't know if Craig will get back in the basketball game—if determination plays a role, I'd place a big bet that he will—but Craig and his family are very much back in the game of life. While they would never have chosen this unexpected challenge, they have all learned to "grow where they're planted." The Huttos, being the warm Southern family they are, are generous in sharing what they've learned.

For starters, they recognize what a miracle it is that Craig survived. The family was at a remote, hard-to-access beach when Craig was attacked. Incredibly, as it turned out, the beach was crawling with medical experts. Three top-notch nurses just happened to be on the beach that morning, as was a doctor and an emergency medical technician. With wonder in her voice, Lou Ann Hutto asks, "What would be the likelihood that that many qualified people would be there at that time, unless it was absolutely meant for him to survive?"[3]

Roger Hutto is still floored by the outpouring of prayers, love, and support that they received from their community and from total strangers. "I just never realized that people could be so caring. We got thousands of cards from people we didn't even know, from all over the country. To me, that somebody stopped and got a card and looked up our address and wrote a card for no other reason than just because they cared—" Roger stops himself, still astonished by the act. "Why, just a few weeks ago, we received something from one of the basketball teams here in Tennessee. It had a check in it for $100 from the team. They said, 'Hey, we are thinking of ya'll, and we wanted to send this to you. Go use it as you see fit.' Does it make any difference?" Roger asks rhetorically. "It may make more impact than you will ever know."[4]

Craig says the cards were a reminder that there are good people in the world. The boost from those notes helped him discover a strength he never knew he had. "I really didn't know I could overcome such a high obstacle. I knew I could overcome things, like, with basketball and baseball and constantly fighting through practice. But this was a life-or-death situation; that's something else." Craig continues, "You don't know what your body can go through until you are put in that position. Your mind and body can be pushed to limits you can't think of. You just have to be strong." Then almost as an afterthought, Craig adds, "Don't give up. You have so much more to offer."

At eighteen, it's way too soon for Craig to know what exactly it is that he has to offer, but he has already seen how his getting back into action has inspired others. He knows he touched a teenage girl who is also an amputee. In tears, she had told Craig how she lay in bed for three months when she lost a limb.

Craig told me, "So much has come from this accident. To tell someone that I didn't give up and hopefully inspire one person, that is the grateful thing for me. As terrible as this was, to inspire one person, that's good."[5]

The Huttos would have never chosen the circumstances in which Craig now finds himself. It would be too much to ask to be content with what Craig has lost. Craig's bedroom is above his parents', and it breaks his dad's heart to hear his son hopping from the bathroom into bed. But the Huttos are dealing with it and know that they will survive. In that regard, it has been the child teaching the parents.

"I think we tend to underestimate a person's spirit. I underestimated Craig," admits Craig's dad, the family worrier. "I have learned and am learning every day. He has helped us through this, a lot more than we've helped him. He's helped me with the psychological things more than I have helped him. The way he copes with it, don't underestimate what a person can do if they are really faced with something."[6]

Craig's mom, Lou Ann, has always made a practice of beginning each day with a thank you prayer. She says her perspective has been refocused on what truly matters. "I tried to do it all. I worked full-time and went above and beyond at work. After this happened, I thought, *I missed so many things while the boys were growing up.* I try to spend more time with my family now than I ever did before."[7]

Once again, Craig is the teacher. First Thessalonians 5:11 says, "Therefore encourage one another, and build up one another . . ." (NASB). It is Craig who is encouraging his mom to go see friends and work out. It is Craig's matter-of-fact way of getting on with life that has helped his father see that he will be OK. It's also Craig who speaks at schools and to civic groups, encouraging others to never give up and to persevere.

The gratitude that Craig and his family are feeling now didn't just begin with thankfulness that he survived his accident. Everyone in the family says, "It's Brian." Brian is the oldest of the Hutto sons, as predisposed to seeing the glass half full as his dad is to worrying about everything. Brian has always been the sunny personality, and his hopefulness permeates the Hutto household.

It could be that the Huttos will all live longer as a result. After all, people who experience positive emotions as children and then later on as adults are half as likely to show high levels of wear and tear on the body.[8]

Most of us aren't challenged by monumental crises like the ones faced by Craig Hutto or Anne Hjelle or Emma Rothbrust. Instead it's the annoying hassles and people that come at us every day that make us go nuts. It's hard to grow where you're planted when the rest of the garden is filled with toxic weeds. Thank You Power can be an excellent weed killer.

Each of us knows people who are just pains in the neck (or

other body parts) and are always able to annoy us. Like anyone in business a long time, Bob Vila has been disappointed more than once by colleagues and associates who've let him down. He's learned to let them go. "There is always the chance that somebody on the team will turn out to be a rat. But there are always other team members who are going to make up for it." Vila has chosen to focus with gratitude on the many people whose dedication makes his business a success, rather than the few who've left him disillusioned.[9]

> *When other people are made to feel important and appreciated, it will no longer be necessary for them to whittle others down in order to be seen bigger by comparison.*
> —Virginia Arcastle

I once had a coworker who constantly poked around on my desk when I wasn't there. Too conflict-adverse for a confrontation, I decided to fill the desk with red herrings: fake memos about important job assignments, meetings with top-level executives, and business trips that would seem to indicate that I was on the fast track. Before long, the snoopy worker casually commented on one of the planted assignments. My suspicions were confirmed, and I realized I'd been done a favor: my colleague's unrestrained curiosity forced me to clean my desk. It became a model of organization, and for that, I remain grateful!

What would happen if you came to work one day and said, "Hello, how are you? I baked cookies last night; want some?" Remember how that bag of candies made the doctors better thinkers? There may be someone who secretly has the dagger out for you, or perhaps he or she is just insecure and, in that insecurity, has been acting like a nitwit. A small gesture directed toward that person costs you little and could change him or her a lot.

For one thing, it makes people more willing to resolve conflict. In one experiment, test subjects were told to sit quietly, make jokes, offer someone candy, or say they were uptight. Then they were put into a dispute that had to be resolved. The people who offered candy or made jokes were more likely to collaborate and work with the other parties to resolve the dispute.[10] Once again, the good feelings from Thank You Power contribute to desired results. And there are many ways to bring Thank You Power to the workplace.

THANK YOU POWER
Embrace your enemy.

For instance, holiday parties can be either a recipe for disaster (think *guy from accounting with a lamp shade on his head*) or an opportunity for real bonding. The in-office party we put together a couple years ago at *Inside Edition* was a real mood booster.

As a television show that covers just about any- and everything, we receive all kinds of free samples of new products and gizmos that companies are trying to get us to feature on the show. Once they're used, we can't send them back, so this particular year, a coworker and I hoarded all the stuff until the Christmas season. With the help of some interns, we stuffed each item into a numbered shopping bag. Each *Inside Edition* staffer drew a number out of a hat and then was made to open his gift bag in front of everyone in the newsroom. Trust me, when the cute guy from graphics opened up a teddy from Victoria's Secret, the place erupted in laughter. The good feelings from that party lasted for weeks. To me anyway, the newsroom—always a high-stress, high-pressure environment—seemed a little less oppressive.

THANK YOU POWER
Look around—what's right with your world?

Take a look at your home, apartment, or dorm room. Look at what you've created. Don't focus on what's *not* right—we all have clutter—but on the things that *are* right. Your hard work and sweat helped create this safe place you call home, no matter how large or small. Give thanks for the strong body that helped you arrange the furniture, the job that helped you pay for it, and the eyes that allow you to see it.

Are there fond memories connected with some of your possessions? Remember the flea-market run when you found that funky picture frame? Relive the moment that's captured in the photograph on the bureau. I remember well my first stereo, which I hung on to for years simply because I worked so hard babysitting and sewing and doing yard work to earn enough to pay for it. I was grateful for that old 8-track, and though it's long gone, the fond feelings I got from earning it are very much with me today.

While you're busy looking over your own place, don't fall victim to the temptation to compare your space to another. There will always be someone with more . . . everything. Whatever the form of measure, comparing how you stack up against others probably won't evoke much Thank You Power.

A study done by Harvard University's Erzo Luttmer used census data to compare happiness levels of people in the same income bracket living in different neighborhoods. The person living in the less-wealthy area was happier.[11] He probably wasn't looking at the neighbors and thinking, *I don't measure up.* His counterpart who lived in the rich side of town probably felt inferior every time he drove through the neighborhood.

If he had passed by the homes of good friends, he might have felt a bit better. As you've learned, the key to Thank You Power is its reminder to us of connections with other people, strengthening the bonds between individuals. People with five or more close friends are 50 percent more likely to describe themselves as "very happy" than those with fewer friends. Are you in a committed relationship or married? Then you're apt to be "very happy." Forty percent of all married couples describe themselves as such.[12]

THANK YOU POWER
Make a list of five people to connect with.

When tragedy struck the Hutto family, they could have been paralyzed by the enormity of what they faced. Instead, they were energized by the encouragement they received from family, friends, and the messages from strangers that flooded the mailbox every day. Thanks to the many people who reached out to the Hutto family; they developed personal relationships that have given them not only moral support but also important information that they've used to figure out what life as an amputee is all about. There's the man from Ohio, who reached out to let them know that Craig's life would go on and be fruitful. He lost a leg at age twenty. He's now married and has two children and a very successful career. Roger and Lou Ann were heartened by his story because it reminded them that Craig still has all those options ahead of him.

Lou Ann also is grateful for the wonderful neighbor she never took time for. "I have a neighbor who's lived here forever." But before the accident, Lou Ann's life was such a whirl that she never even noticed this nice woman. "She came over after the accident, and we have become friends."[13]

Look in your own address book. There are dozens of names of people you call friends, yet you never phone them. Make a point to change that. My recent high-school reunion allowed me to reconnect with men and women I hadn't seen for years. Despite the distance of miles and time, many of us realized that we had an amazing amount of experiences in common. Thanks to e-mail, we've kept in contact. It has cost us nothing but time, and I feel much richer because of it.

One of those connections could be right under your nose.

Cara Mia Jones is a promotions coordinator at an Atlanta television station. As part of her job, she tries to get the station's on-air team and community service projects noticed. She'd limited her radio efforts primarily to stations that advertised on her television station. When an out-of-town visitor suggested that other stations would probably be thrilled to jazz up their shows with the station's talent, she took advantage of the tip. After a couple of lunches with executives at some additional stations, she's now secured a regular monthly appearance for some of her talent. She's hopeful that it will translate into ratings points for her station. As it turns out, some of the radio producers she's called on are turning out to be closer personal friends.

Cara says that that visitor's suggestion was the kick in the pants she needed. "I knew I had it in me all along; it just sparked something. I have made a marketing plan for the station," she says, and she's moving forward from there. She's also struck by the fact that the advice came from someone who personally benefited in no way.

"They are doing it out of the kindness of their hearts," she explains. "It just gives you faith in humanity that there are nice souls out there who are willing to help for no other reason than selflessness and wanting others to succeed as well."

Remember earlier in the book, when we talked about how grateful people are more willing to do for others? A few months after Cara got what she calls that *kick in the pants*, she was on a plane, chatting with the flight attendant. "I mentioned that my career was going well and I was right on track. She said she had a daughter my age that could use some direction." So Cara gave the woman her business card and suggested her daughter give her a call.

> *It is amazing what you can accomplish if you do not care who gets the credit.*
> —HARRY TRUMAN

The two young women eventually met for lunch, and Cara now says with pride that she's helping her new friend get into a career that suits her personality. The promotions coordinator who was on the receiving end of advice just a few months before is now eagerly dispensing it herself. Filled with thanks for her unexpected advisor, Cara is now using Thank You Power to help her new friend.

"She's my age," Cara relates, "but she really hasn't done much in the four years since college. But all my advice has helped her, and she is on her way to a career that will be fulfilling." Cara marvels herself at the notion that someone still relatively new to the work world is able to give career guidance. Her just-move-ahead-with-life attitude helps her make sense of it. She says, "I just figured even if I've only been in it a few years, a little advice can still help someone else trying to find themselves and what they want to do."

Cara couldn't be more excited, and though she never expected that *she'd* benefit from helping her young friend, she tells me she has. "I have found that the more you help people out of the kindness of your heart, the better life is. It just makes getting up in the morning all the better!"[14]

Imagine! A total stranger helps a total stranger because a total stranger helped her. Cara Mia Jones is living proof that Thank You Power encourages people to extend themselves on behalf of others.

THANK YOU POWER
Help someone outside your comfort zone.

nine

What's *Your* Tagline?

> *The way to gain a good reputation is to endeavor to be what you desire to appear.*
>
> —SOCRATES

IF YOU WERE A PRODUCT, WHAT WORDS WOULD BE USED by your promoters to market you? They call them taglines in advertising: quick, pithy words or phrases that sum up the product or service in less than a sound bite. Some still resonate years after they've been put to bed. "*I can't believe I ate the whole thing*" was exactly what 1970s TV watchers said before plopping a couple of Alka-Seltzers into a glass of water. In the same decade, "You've come a long way, baby" sold Virginia Slims cigarettes and feminized smoking. More recently, Nike's "Just Do It" urged people to start moving, and to wear Nike sneakers as they did. Dodge trucks urged consumers to "grab life by the horns," a tagline that communicated boldness, adventure, and ruggedness—all qualities the typical truck buyer would presumably see in himself.

Sometimes the taglines change because the business has evolved. General Electric, which for years said, "We bring good things to life" has recently retired that line in favor of "imagination at work," underscoring the brainpower that runs throughout GE's disparate businesses.

Your tagline is more than just an advertising slogan. It is shorthand for the motto by which you live, a bumper sticker that guides you forward. A big rig may have a sticker that tells you, "I brake at railroad crossings." Try to boil it down to one single phrase and you'll start pulling your hair out. You'll also understand why those advertising people make so much money. Those short, clever lines are harder to come up with than you'd think!

Among my bumper stickers is "Moving On"—meaning I try to just keep one foot in front of the other, moving forward in my life's journey. Many days I hear, "This, Too, Shall Pass"—words that my late mother often said to remind me that whatever it is, it won't last. And I often find myself mentally asking, *Where's the Thank You Power?*—a reminder to look for the blessings in every situation because they are there.

But my personal tagline is "Here to Make a Difference." I have never for a moment believed that life was just a series of days, and then you die. I believe we were meant to experience as much as we have the opportunity to, and to have meaningful connections with the people around us. I think that when we leave this earth, something about it should be better for our having been here.

There are so many ways to make that difference, which is really what Thank You Power is all about. Doing something for someone else makes both of you feel good. The broaden-and-build aspect of feeling good makes you more adventurous and more inclined to try the new things that make life invigorating. The new experiences give you memories that, when recalled, lift you up even more.[1] It's an upward spiral that all starts with Thank You Power.

Professor Alice Isen, the Cornell psychologist who researched what happens when people feel good, says that Thank You Power makes you stronger. "You are a stronger person and more resilient to negative forces," she says. "People are more likely to do what they want to do when they are in positive affect." She says it's conceivable that people with self-esteem issues might become more assertive if they put Thank You Power to work.[2] For example, focusing on that one happy moment can help a child perform better on a test.

THANK YOU POWER
What do you stand for?

I know the changes that I've made in my own life since I started following that hunch that hit me. If I really am "Here to Make a Difference," then Sal Morales is my proof that one can. His gratitude-infused outlook helped revive his television career. If Sal had a tagline, I think it would be "I have value." Over the last several months, Sal has allowed himself to reconnect with all those fine qualities he'd forgotten he had. Take a peek at another e-mail message he just sent to me:

I have learned that what I have is called *talent*, that it is truly a gift. I have learned that if given the opportunity, I can produce positive results in any aspect. I am good at what I do. I am a good person, I don't hurt others, I am fun, and energetic, a good brother, son, nephew, cousin, uncle. I didn't know that.[3]

As you read those incredibly uplifting words, can you believe they were written by a man who just lost his job—again? That's right. I was almost as stunned as Sal to learn that budget cutbacks at the station had meant the dismantling of Sal's department. It is so sad when you think about it. Sal says in just eight short months, the "little station that could" earned eighteen Emmy nominations, including that very special nomination that had Sal Morales's name on it.[4] Yet Sal isn't mourning. The difference between the way he's handled this job setback compared to the one before is like night and day. Someone who saw Sal the other day described him as happy, content, assertive, and animated. Hardly the description of a defeated individual.

What's different this time? He says, "Life, I have learned, is nothing more than a series of events or chapters. And the chapter I wrote last year was with God's pen, so to speak." Sal says, rereading that chapter, he sees how much he learned and how much he has to offer the next station lucky enough (my words, not Sal's!) to get him. Thank You Power helped bring Sal Morales back from a very dark place to a life of optimism and joy, even during rough spots like this.

Thank You Power *and*—Sal suspects—something else. "Some force, God, Jesus? I really don't know," he muses. "Something out there did lead me back. And from it," he concludes, "I got a sense of self."[5]

But what about the people manning the front lines of Thank You Power, the men and women who've spent years studying gratitude and positive emotion? Has the study of Thank You Power meant anything outside the research lab? Not surprisingly, the answer is yes.

Robert Emmons, the University of California–Davis professor who coauthored that groundbreaking catalog of the benefits of daily gratitude, says that practicing what he's studied has made a huge impact in his own life. "I came more from the side of the whining, complaining group. You know, the people who have a sense of entitlement or deservingness. I think gratitude has helped me shift my own frame of reference. It has really made a difference in my life."[6] The man who wanted to see from a scientific perspective if "we could make people more grateful" has become more grateful himself.

Chris Peterson, whose work in the field has helped identify gratitude as one of the most fulfilling of all the character strengths he helped categorize, says, "I am more mindful of what is positive in other people. I am still struggling with what's positive in myself. I suppose I am one of those 'hardworking, never-quite-good-enough' kinds of people. I think people who achieve are like that."

But Peterson has seen a difference in himself that he says other people have actually commented on. "I am much more overtly kind to people," he shares. "I was never a mean person, but I had a relatively sharp tongue. I don't at all anymore! I just say a lot of 'please' and 'thank you.' It's like I went back to kindergarten," he concludes with a laugh.

"Do you like yourself better?" I quizzed.

"Absolutely," he answered emphatically, with a chuckle. "It's more fun to get along with people. Why does it take so long to figure that out?"[7]

Jon Haidt, who has studied elevation, that good feeling the rest of us get from hearing about good things done for someone else, says he's been changed by his work. "I took the strengths test [developed by Chris Peterson and his colleagues] and found that gratitude is one of my weakest points. My wife is one of the most grateful people, and even though I didn't think I was ungrateful, I learned I wasn't particularly grateful. So now I make more of an effort to express my thanks. I make a bit more of an effort to express my appreciation."[8]

Philip Watkins at Eastern Washington University had a similar discovery. "One of the consequences of studying gratitude," he told me, "is learning how really ungrateful I am! When I look at what I have in my life, I should be more grateful and complain a lot less."

The realization forced a change in Dr. Watkins's life. "I think studying gratitude helps me notice the simple pleasures in my life. I am better at noticing them. Other than my religious activities, which encourage me to regularly take stock, I don't regularly sit down and count my blessings. I tend to do it more naturally, though I don't disparage an exercise of doing this."[9]

Barbara Fredrickson, broadening and building her repertoire of Thank You Power says, "It changes the way you look at the world." She explains, "One key piece of gratitude is that it basically has the potential to change everything from its ordinary state to being a gift. Once you see it as a gift, it changes the emotional connection to it."

Fredrickson says the longer she works in this field, the more amazed she is by the power of thank you. "I think I've become more stunned over the years. I have more of a sense of awe than when you first get to the tip of the iceberg and you don't really know where it's going to lead. Now I look and see this larger stream of evidence of how this works in these different ways, and it's, like, wow!"[10]

The wow factor is what's kept Alice Isen going for all these years too. "I am happy to have discovered something that is true, first of all," she says, choosing her words carefully. "I feel happy to be able to tell people to enjoy happiness, to show the benefits of it. I am especially happy if I can point out to people how beneficial small things can be in their lives, how beneficial small, positive events in their lives can be to their thinking, to their interpersonal relationships, to their way of being in the world."[11]

I can relate. It is awe-inspiring to see someone put Thank You Power to work. You've seen how it has worked both in the research labs and in real life. There is still one place yet to apply it: your own life. Give it a shot. After trying Thank You Power, I suspect that you, too, will find yourself saying thank you.

ten

A Special Message for People of Faith

*God causes all things to work together
for good to those who love God.*

—ROMANS 8:28 (NASB)

If you are a person of faith, it is impossible to talk about gratitude without mentioning the source of all things in life—our Creator. In every great religion on the planet, thanksgiving plays an important role. That is not by accident.

People of faith have long known the rejuvenating possibilities of Thank You Power. Duke University research has found that religious people generally have a positive view of the world and are more likely to feel grateful. Researchers at Duke have also found that under stressful situations, religious people cope better.[1]

Religious people are also happier. Since 1972, the Pew Research Center has been polling on this subject and has proved overwhelmingly that people who attend services are just happier people. Only 26 percent of those who rarely or never attend religious services describe themselves as "very happy." But 46 percent of those who attend religious services at least once a week say they are very happy.[2]

Psychology professor Robert Emmons explains why he thinks that is: "I think religion gives a much broader base for their gratitude. In religious faith, it positions it within a historical tradition that every religion in the world places a high premium on gratefulness. There are prayers in every tradition that are exclusively focused on giving thanks. It gives a person more strategies and tactics and ultimately more reasons to be thankful." He also says, "It gets you back to where things came from. It has an almost cosmic quest to it."[3]

That quest is resonating with a lot of people, who see benefit in expressing thanks to a higher power. In a 1998

> *I will give you a new heart and put a new spirit within you; I will take the heart of stone out of your flesh and give you a heart of flesh.*
> —EZEKIEL 36:26 (NKJV)

Gallup survey of 482 adults and 500 teens, 78 percent of teenagers and 89 percent of adults express gratitude to a god or creator "all of the time" or "some of the time."[4]

That's my style. While I do have a specific time to count my blessings, Thank You Power is a round-the-clock endeavor for me. God and I have quick conversations, just a line or two, all day. I think of it as instant-messaging . . . without the computer. I don't have digital records of our chats, but I know they are happening just the same.

Anne Hjelle, the biker who was attacked by a mountain lion, knows that God had an enormous role in her near-death experience. She says she has seen too many signs of His hand at work not to believe that. In fact, even before the attack, she feels that God was laying the groundwork for her survival. "We had a woman in

> *Faith is the substance of things hoped for, the evidence of things not seen.*
> —HEBREWS 11:1 (KJV)

our church that two days before this happened, God told her to 'pray for protection from mountain lions,'" Anne says, with a bit of wonder in her voice. "She is running, you know, her daily jog, and she gets this very strong impression that she should pray about this. She thought, *That's so weird!*" So that day she prayed for protection from mountain lions. She had no idea [who] for. The next day, she said she prayed, 'God, we need a miracle.'"

Anne is a member of a group called the Trail Angels, Christian women who share a love of mountain biking. At the precise moment that Anne was being attacked, one of her Trail Angel friends biking in a different section of the park had an experience that, at the time, she couldn't understand. Reaching a certain point on her trail, she just suddenly stopped and started crying. She didn't know why. She then read a biblical affirmation taped to the top tube of her bike: "I believe the Lord is my strength."

The friend went back to the park a few weeks later, rode the section of trail that Anne had been riding, and timed it out to compare to the point at which she was overcome by tears: she had stopped at the same time that Anne was attacked!

But the biggest miracle of all may have been the heroics of

Debi Nicholls. It is because of her that John 15:13 has such meaning: "Greater love has no one than this, than to lay down one's life for his friends" (NKJV). And for Anne Hjelle, 2 Timothy 4:17 has literal meaning: "But the Lord stood with me and strengthened me . . . I was delivered out of the mouth of the lion" (NKJV). Anne is confident that God saved her from the lion for a higher purpose. "I *do* know what my purpose is," she says. "It's to share with others what I have learned through my experiences, so that they can gain the benefit of the knowledge without the pain of the struggle."[5]

THANK YOU POWER
Give thanks to God.

Psalm 118:1 says, "Give thanks to the LORD, for He is good; for His lovingkindness is everlasting" (NASB). Whenever I have talked with God, He has listened. And He has always answered. I may not have *heard* the answer or may not have *liked* the one I got, but it was there.

Since I began trying to incorporate Thank You Power into my own life, it somehow seems that the conversations with God go easier. I am sure the difference is with me, not Him. Whether in my spiritual journey or just in my struggles to get through yet another action-packed day, with more to do than there is time to do it, Thank You Power seems to help. It's the emery board that smoothes off the rough edges. The grease that makes the wheels spin more smoothly. It is that deep breath of crisp, clean air that makes me think more clearly in the early morning. It all starts with those two words: *thank you*.

If you are ready for miracles, if you think that life has something more to offer you and that now is the time to enjoy all of life's blessings, say thank you.

If you long to experience greater joy each day, a deeper peace during the quiet moments, and a closer, more fulfilling relationship with your loved ones than you have right now, say thank you.

If you want to enjoy all the joy and happiness, not only to which you are entitled but also that *God wants for you*, say thank you.

The power to have it all is right in those two little words. For that, I join you in saying . . . thank you.

appendix

Values in Action—
Strengths of Character[1]

STRENGTHS OF WISDOM AND KNOWLEDGE

- ♦ Creativity (Originality, Ingenuity)
- ♦ Curiosity (Interest)
- ♦ Active Open-Mindedness (Judgment, Critical Thinking)
- ♦ Love of Learning
- ♦ Perspective (Wisdom)

STRENGTHS OF COURAGE

- ♦ Bravery (Valor)
- ♦ Industry (Perseverance, Diligence)
- ♦ Honesty (Authenticity, Sincerity, Integrity)
- ♦ Vitality (Vigor, Zest, Enthusiasm)

STRENGTHS OF HUMANITY

- ♦ Intimate Attachment (Capacity to Love and Be Loved)
- ♦ Kindness (Altruism, Generosity, Nurturance, Care, "Niceness")
- ♦ Hot Intelligence

STRENGTHS OF JUSTICE

- ◆ Citizenship and Teamwork (Duty, Social Responsibility, Loyalty)
- ◆ Fairness (Justice, Equity)
- ◆ Leadership

STRENGTHS OF TEMPERANCE

- ◆ Forgiveness and Mercy
- ◆ Modesty and Humility
- ◆ Prudence
- ◆ Regulation of Oneself (Self-Control, Self-Discipline)

STRENGTHS OF TRANSCENDENCE

- ◆ Appreciation of Beauty and Excellence (Awe, Wonder)
- ◆ Gratitude
- ◆ Hope (Optimism, Future-Mindedness, Future Orientation)
- ◆ Playfulness and Humor
- ◆ Spirituality (Religiousness, Sense of Purpose)

Take the online test to find your signature strengths at
www.authentichappiness.org.

Acknowledgments

WE LEARN WHAT WE SEE. I WAS PRIVILEGED FROM MY earliest days to have two parents who believed that there was honor in hard work, that there were no shortcuts to success, and that even in adversities there were blessings to be found. To my late mother, Merle Olson Norville, and my dad, Zack Norville, thank you for it all: the spankings, the lectures, the adventures, and the love. I hope I've done you proud with the way I've lived my life.

To my sisters Nancy, Cathy, and Patti: Who knew that the little girls with whom I shared a childhood of snatched Barbie dolls, Kick the Can, dog baths, and car washes would turn into such awesome women? Despite the miles, you are always there for me, and I say thank you for you daily.

The completion of this book prompts a long and gratitude-filled thank you list. I am grateful for the dynamic duo from Dallas, my literary agents, Jan Miller and Shannon Miser-Marven of Dupree-Miller. Jan, you could fill a room with your energy, and your enthusiasm for this project has been a much-needed boost when I felt as if I was running out of steam. Shannon, your guidance and advice have been invaluable each step of the way. I say thank you to you both though it hardly seems enough. Thanks as well to the team at Thomas Nelson Publishing, from Jonathan

Merkh, who first saw the power of thank you, to Kristen Parrish, Paula Major, Joey Paul, and Tami Heim, who saw this book through to completion. Your support, enthusiasm, and dedication have been wonderful.

To the experts and individuals who so generously agreed to be interviewed for this book, I appreciate your sharing your stories. A special thank you to the psychologists for your time and care in reviewing this material: your research enlightens all of us, and I am grateful to be able to share it with a wider audience. Lindsey Wisniewski, you did an amazing job tracking down all the research I needed for this project. You'll be an awesome lawyer.

My children, Niki, Kyle, and Mikaela, give me reason to say thank you every day. Alsklings, your incredibly bright minds, delicious senses of humor, and unlimited love and kindness bring joy to my life every single minute. I don't know how I got so lucky to be your mom, but I am eternally grateful because of it.

And Karl. Thank you for it all. For those fabulous children, for the amazingly interesting and varied life we've created, for the nights you let me stay up late and didn't complain when I got up early to squeeze in some writing, thank you. Had you not read the early versions of this and said, "Keep going; this is important," this book would remain unwritten. You were the spark that helped me ignite *Thank You Power*. Twenty years ago, a minister asked, "Do you take . . . ?" I still do.

Finally, to God. You have blessed me beyond imagination and hear, "Thank You," from me every day. You've got me here for a purpose. With Your help, I'll fulfill it.

Notes

INTRODUCTION

1. National Opinion Research Center, University of Chicago.
2. Daniel Kahneman, et al., "Would You Be Happier If You Were Richer? A Focusing Illusion," *Science*, June 30, 2006, as reported in *Money* magazine, July 18, 2006.

ONE: THE POWER OF *THANK YOU*

1. David Patrick Columbia, personal interview by author, November 20, 2006.
2. Roy F. Baumeister and Stacey A. Ilko, "Shallow Gratitude: Public and Private Acknowledgement of External Help in Accounts of Success," *Basic and Applied Social Psychology* 16 (1995), 191–209.
3. Maya Pines, "A Secret Sense in the Human Nose: Pheromones and Mammals," www.hhmi.org/senses/d230.html.
4. Robert A. Emmons, telephone interview by author, October 17, 2006.
5. Robert A. Emmons and Michael E. McCullough, "Counting Blessings versus Burdens: Experimental Studies of Gratitude and Subjective Well-Being in Daily Life," *Journal of Personality and Social Psychology* 84, no. 2 (2003), 377–89; see also Michael E. McCullough, Robert A. Emmons, and Jo-Ann

Tsang, "The Grateful Disposition: A Conceptual and Empirical Topography," *Journal of Personality and Social Psychology* 82, no. 1 (January 2002), 112–27; and Michael E. McCullough, Shelley D. Kilpatrick, and Robert A. Emmons, "Is Gratitude a Moral Affect?" *Psychological Bulletin* 127, no. 2 (March 2001), 249–66.

6. Emmons, telephone interview by author, October 17, 2006.

7. Emmons and McCullough, "Counting Blessings versus Burdens."

8. A. M. Isen, "The Influence of Positive and Negative Affect on Cognitive Organization: Some Implications for Development," in Nancy L. Stein, Bennett Leventhal, and Tom Trabasso (eds.), *Psychological and Biological Approaches to Emotion* (Hillsdale, NJ: Erlbaum, 1990), 75–94.

9. Barbara L. Fredrickson, "The Role of Positive Emotions on Positive Psychology: The Broaden-and-Build Theory of Positive Emotions," *American Psychologist* 56, no. 3 (2001), 218–26.

10. David A. Padgett and R. Glaser, "How Stress Influences the Immune Response," *Trends in Immunology* 24, no. 8 (2003), 444–48. This study looked at the physiological impact of stress on the immune system.

11. Deborah Danner, David Snowden, and Wallace Friesen, "Positive Emotions in Early Life and Longevity: Findings from the Nun Study," *Journal of Personal and Social Psychiatry* 80, no. 5 (2001), 804–13.

12. It is not clear whether increased religiousness is an end product of grateful thinking or if religious people simply tend to be more grateful.

13. Emmons, telephone interview by author, October 17, 2006.

14. S. Graham and B. Weiner, "From an Attributional Theory of

Emotion to Developmental Psychology: A Round Trip Ticket?" *Social Cognition* 4 (1986), 152–79.

15. Emmons, telephone interview by author, October 17, 2006.

16. S. Lyubomirsky, C. Tkach, and J. Yelverton, "Pursuing Sustained Happiness Through Random Acts of Kindness and Counting One's Blessings: Tests of Two Six-Week Interventions," University of California–Riverside, Department of Psychology, 2004.

17. Jonathan W. Schooler, Daniel Ariely, and George Loewenstein, "The Pursuit and Assessment of Happiness May Be Self-Defeating," in *The Psychology of Economic Decisions*, J. Carrillo and I. Brocas, eds. (Oxford University Press, 2003).

18. Jim Boyles, personal interview by author, October 19, 2006.

19. Mrs. Jim Boyles, personal interview by author, October 19, 2006.

TWO: HELLO, *THANK YOU*, MY OLD FRIEND

1. Alice Isen, telephone interview by author, November 11, 2006.

2. Ibid.

3. Online Etymology Dictionary, s.v. "gratitude," etymonline.com.

4. Dictionary.com, s.v. "thank."

5. Koran 14:7.

6. 1 Thessalonians 5:16–18 (NKJV).

7. Psalm 118:24 (KJV).

8. Buddhist text.

9. Sonya Lyubomirsky, Laura King, and Ed Diener, "The Benefits of Frequent Positive Affect: Does Happiness Lead to Success?" *Psychological Bulletin* 131, no. 6 (2005), 803–55.

10. Robert A. Emmons, Michael E. McCullough, and Jo-Ann Tsang, "The Grateful Disposition: A Conceptual and Empirical Topography," *Journal of Personality and Social*

Psychology 82, no. 1 (2002), 112–27; the Gratitude Questionnaire (GQ-6) was revised slightly from the original version presented in the Emmons, McCullough, Tsang research for its inclusion in this book.

11. Chris Peterson, telephone interview by author, October 16, 2006.

12. Christopher Peterson and Martin E. P. Seligman, *Character Strengths and Virtues: A Handbook and Classification* (Washington, DC: American Psychological Association and Oxford University Press, 2004), 20.

13. Christopher Peterson, Nansook Park, and Martin E. P. Seligman, "Orientations to Happiness and Life Satisfaction: The Full Life Versus the Empty Life," *Journal of Happiness Studies* 6 (March 2005), 25–41.

14. Megan Mahoney, telephone interview by author, October 31, 2006.

15. A. M. Isen, et al., "Affect, Accessibility of Material in Memory and Behavior: A Cognitive Loop?" *Journal of Personality and Social Psychology* 36, no. 1 (1978), 1–12; see also F. Gregory Ashby, Alice M. Isen, and U. Turken, "A neuropsychological theory of positive affect and its influence on cognition," *Psychological Review* (1999), 106, 529–50; C. Estrada, M. Young, and Alice M. Isen, "Positive affect influences creative problem solving and reported source of practice satisfaction in physicians," *Motivation and Emotion* (1994), 18, 285–99; and Alice M. Isen, K. A. Daubman, and G. P. Nowicki, "Positive affect facilitates creative problem solving," *Journal of Personality and Social Psychology* (1987), 52, 1122–31.

16. John C. Masters, R. C. Barden, and M. E. Ford, "Affective States, Expressive Behavior and Learning in Children,"

Journal of Personality and Social Psychiatry 37, no. 3 (1979), 380–90.

17. Isen, telephone interview by author, November 11, 2006.
18. J. M. George, "State or Trait: Effects of Positive Mood on Prosocial Behavior at Work," *Journal of Applied Psychology* 76, vol. 2 (1991), 299–307.
19. George, "Salesperson Mood at Work: Implications for Helping Customers," *Journal of Personal Selling and Sales Management* 17, no. 3 (1998), 23–30.

THREE: DON'T SWEAT THE SMALL STUFF—NOTICE IT!

1. Whitney Toombs, personal interview by author, October 31, 2006.
2. Neal Feldman, personal interview by author, November 18, 2006.
3. Ann Rubenstein Tisch, personal interview by author, November 17, 2006.
4. Rene Sanchez, "In East Harlem, a School Without Boys: Experiment with All-Girl Classes Taps New Mood in Public Education," *Washington Post*, September 22, 1996.
5. Tisch personal interview, ibid.
6. Aron Ralston, in-studio interview by author, *Deborah Norville Tonight*, MSNBC Cable Network, September 16, 2004.
7. Donna Davis, telephone interview by author, November 15, 2006.
8. Philip Hilder, telephone interview by author, November 24, 2006.
9. Philip Watkins, telephone interview by author, October 18, 2006.
10. Hilder telephone interview, ibid.

FOUR: ACCENTUATE THE POSITIVE

1. Anne Hjelle, April 19, 2004 interview by author, *Inside Edition*, syndicated television magazine, May 3 and 4, 2004.
2. Debi Nicholls, April 15, 2004 interview, *Inside Edition*, syndicated television magazine, May 3 and 4, 2004.
3. Hjelle interview, ibid.
4. Ibid.
5. Barbara L. Fredrickson, Roberta A. Mancuso, Christine Branigan, and Michele M. Tugade, "The Undoing Effect of Positive Emotions," *Motion and Emotion* 24, no. 4 (2000), 237–58.
6. Barbara L. Fredrickson, telephone interview by author, November 2, 2006.
7. Barbara L. Fredrickson and Robert W. Levenson, "Positive Emotions Speed Recovery from the Cardiovascular Sequelae of Negative Emotions," *Cognition and Emotion* 12, no. 2 (1998), 191–220.
8. Fredrickson, telephone interview by author, November 2, 2006.
9. Ibid.
10. Fredrickson and Robert W. Levenson, "Positive Emotions Speed Recovery from the Cardio-Vascular Sequelae of Negative Emotions," ibid; see also Barbara L. Fredrickson and Christine Branigan, "Positive Emotions Broaden Scope of Attention and Thought-Action Repertoires," *Cognition and Emotion* 19, no. 3 (2005), 313–32; Michele M. Tugade, Barbara L. Fredrickson, Lisa F. Barrett, "Psychological Resilience and Positive Emotional Granularity: Examining the Benefits of Positive Emotions on Coping and Health," *Journal of Personality* 72, no. 6 (December 2004), 1161–90; Barbara L. Fredrickson, "The Value of Positive Emotions," *American*

Scientist 91 (2003), 330–35; and Barbara L. Fredrickson, "What Good Are Positive Emotions?" *Review of General Psychology* 2, no. 3 (1998), 300–19.

11. Philip C. Watkins, Dean L. Grimm, and Russell Kolts, "Counting Your Blessings: Positive Memories Among Grateful Persons," *Current Psychology* 23, no. 1 (Spring 2004), 52–67; see also Philip C. Watkins, J. Scheer, M. Ovnicek, and Russell D. Kolts, "The debt of gratitude: Dissociating gratitude and indebtedness," *Cognition and Emotion* 20 (2006), 217–41; Philip C. Watkins, Michael Van Gelder, and Laden Maleki, *Counting (and recalling) blessings: Trait gratitude predicts positive memory bias* (August 2006), presentation to the annual convention of the American Psychological Association, New Orleans, LA; also telephone interview by author, October 25, 2006.

12. Anne Hjelle, personal interview by author, April 19, 2004.

13. Watkins, telephone interview by author, October 25, 2006.

14. Hjelle, e-mail communication to author, February 5, 2007.

15. Watkins telephone interview, ibid.

FIVE: GIVE THANKS FOR THE BAD—PRAISE YOUR PROBLEMS

1. Emma Rothbrust, telephone interview by author, November 1, 2006.

2. Ibid.

3. Emma Rothbrust, e-mail communication to author, January 31, 2007.

4. Barbara L. Fredrickson, et al., "What Good Are Positive Emotions in Crises? A Prospective Study of Resilience and Emotions Following the Terrorist Attacks on the United States

on September 11, 2001," *Journal of Personality and Social Psychology* 84, no. 2 (2003), 365–76.

5. Ellen Niven, personal interview by author, December 2, 2006.

6. Todd B. Kashdan, Gitendra Uswatte, and Terri Julian, "Gratitude and Hedonic and Eudaimonic Well-Being in Vietnam War Veterans," *Behaviour Research and Therapy* 44 (2006), 177–99.

7. Deborah Danner, David Snowden, and Wallace Friesen, "Positive Emotions in Early Life and Longevity," *Journal of Personality and Social Psychology* 80 (2001), 804–13.

8. Philip C. Watkins, Dean L. Grimm, and Russell Kolts, "Counting Your Blessings: Positive Memories Among Grateful Persons," *Current Psychology* 23, no. 1 (2004), 52–67.

9. Watkins, telephone interview by author, October 26, 2006.

10. Chuck Adams, telephone interview by author, October 8, 2006.

11. Ibid.

SIX: STOP STARING IN THE MIRROR—LOOK OUT THE WINDOW INSTEAD

1. Sal Morales, telephone interview by author, November 6, 2006.

2. Ibid.

3. www.dnorville.com/chat/gratitude.php.

4. Morales telephone interview, ibid.

5. Ibid.

6. Morales, e-mail communication to author, September 2, 2006.

7. Morales, e-mail communication to author, October 30, 2006.

8. Morales telephone interview, ibid.

9. J. Silvers and J. Haidt (under review), "Moral Elevation Can Induce Lactation," (unpublished manuscript, University of Virginia).

10. Jonathan Haidt, telephone interview by author, October 12, 2006; see also Jonathan Haidt, *The Happiness Hypothesis: Finding Modern Truth in Ancient Wisdom* (Basic Books, 2006).

11. L. P. McGovern, J. L. Ditzian, and S. P. Taylor, "The Effect of Positive Reinforcement on Helping with Cost," *Psychonomic Society Bulletin* 5 (1975), 421–23.

12. Hewitt B. Clark, J. T. Northrop, and C. T. Barkshire, "The Effects of Contingent Thank-You Notes on Case Managers' Visiting Residential Clients," *Education and Treatment of Children* 11, no. 1 (1988), 45–51.

13. Bruce Rind and Prashant Bordia, "Effect of Server's 'Thank You' and Personalization on Restaurant Tipping," *Journal of Applied Social Psychiatry* 25, no. 9 (1995), 745–51.

14. Bruce Rind and David Strohmetz, "Effect on Restaurant Tipping of a Helpful Message Written on the Back of Customers' Checks," *Journal of Applied Social Psychiatry* 29, no. 1 (1999), 139–44.

15. J. Ronald Carey, Steven H. Clicque, Barbara A. Leighton, Frank Milton, "A Test of Positive Reinforcement of Customers," *Journal of Marketing* 40, no. 4 (October 1976), 98–100; doi:10.2307/1251075.

16. Kim Keough, e-mail communication to author, November 15, 2006.

17. Ibid.

18. Henry David Thoreau, *Walden* (New York: Houghton Mifflin, 1949), 87.

SEVEN: YOUR SECRET GARDEN

1. Lily Chin, telephone interview by author, November 29, 2006. For more information on the Red Scarf Project, visit www.orphan.org.

2. See appendix for complete Values in Strength list.

3. Christopher Peterson and Martin E. P. Seligman, *Character Strengths and Virtues: A Handbook and Classification* (Oxford University Press and American Psychological Association, 2004).

4. Martin E. P. Seligman, "Teaching Positive Psychology," *APA Monitor* 30, no. 7 (July/August 1999).

5. Bob Vila, telephone interview by author, November 30, 2006.

6. Ibid.

EIGHT: GROW WHERE YOU'RE PLANTED

1. Craig Hutto, telephone interview by author, November 13, 2006.

2. Lou Ann Hutto, telephone interview by author, November 13, 2006.

3. Ibid.

4. Roger Hutto, telephone interview by author, November 13, 2006.

5. Craig Hutto telephone interview, ibid.

6. Roger Hutto telephone interview, ibid.

7. Lou Ann Hutto telephone interview, ibid.

8. C. D. Ryff, et al., "Elective Affinities and Uninvited Agonies," in C. D. Ryff and B. H. Singer, eds., *Emotion, Social Relationships, and Health* (New York: Oxford University Press, 2001).

9. Vila, telephone interview by author, November 30, 2006.

10. M. Carlson, V. Charlin, and N. Miller, "Positive Mood and Helping Behavior: A Test of Six Hypotheses," *Journal of Personality and Social Psychology* 55, no. 2 (August 1988), 211–29.

11. Erzo F. P. Luttmer, "Neighbors as Negatives: Relative Earnings

and Well-Being," *Quarterly Journal of Economics* 120, no. 3 (August 2005), 963–1002.

12. The General Social Survey, conducted by the National Opinion Research Center of the University of Chicago. Since 1972, the GSS has been regularly polling married Americans on the state of their marriage.

13. Lou Ann Hutto telephone interview, ibid.

14. Cara Mia Jones, telephone interview by author, November 5, 2006.

NINE: WHAT'S *YOUR* TAGLINE?

1. Barbara L. Fredrickson, "The Role of Positive Emotions on Positive Psychology: The Broaden-and-Build Theory of Positive Emotions," *American Psychologist* 56, no. 3 (2001), 218–26.

2. Isen, telephone interview by author, November 11, 2006.

3. Morales, e-mail communication to author, February 5, 2007.

4. Ibid.

5. Ibid.

6. Emmons, telephone interview by author, October 17, 2006.

7. Peterson, telephone interview by author, October 16, 2006.

8. Haidt, telephone interview by author, October 12, 2006.

9. Watkins, telephone interview by author, October 25, 2006.

10. Fredrickson, telephone interview by author, November 2, 2006.

11. Isen, telephone interview by author, November 11, 2006.

TEN: A SPECIAL MESSAGE FOR PEOPLE OF FAITH

1. H. G. Koenig, et al., "Does religious attendance prolong survival? A six-year follow-up study of 3,968 older adults," *Journal of Gerontology* 54 (July/August 1999), 370–77; a study

of nearly four thousand elderly North Carolinians found that those who attended religious services weekly were 46 percent less likely to die over a six-year period than those who attended less or not at all.

2. "Are We Happy Yet?" Pew Research Center Publications, 1615 L Street, NW, Suite 700, Washington, DC 20036, February 13, 2006; www.pewresearch.org.

3. Emmons, telephone interview by author, October 17, 2006.

4. Gallup Poll, *April Wave* 1, April 17–19, 1998.

5. Hjelle, e-mail communication to author, February 6, 2007.

APPENDIX: VALUES IN ACTION—STRENGTHS OF CHARACTER

1. Christopher Peterson and Martin E. P. Seligman, *Character Strengths and Virtues: A Handbook and Classification* (Oxford University Press and American Psychological Association, 2004).

About the Author

DEBORAH NORVILLE is the anchor of *Inside Edition*, the nation's longest-running syndicated television magazine. The two-time Emmy Award winner is a summa cum laude graduate of the University of Georgia and began her television career at WAGA-TV in Atlanta while still a college student. Formerly the coanchor of NBC's *Today*, Deborah has reported and anchored for WMAQ-TV in Chicago, NBC News, CBS News, and MSNBC and hosted a national radio show for ABC Radio. Deborah is also a best-selling author. Her titles include *Back on Track: How to Straighten Out Your Life When It Throws You a Curve*, *I Don't Want to Sleep Tonight*, and *I Can Fly*.

She and her husband, Karl Wellner, live in New York City with their three children. Deborah can be reached via her Web site: **www.dnorville.com.**

You can learn more about putting
Thank You Power in your life by visiting
www.thankyoupower.net.